THE ODYSSEY
OF
HOMER

Odysseus

AN ADAPTED CLASSIC

THE ODYSSEY
OF
HOMER

HOMER

Adapted by
Henry I. Christ

GLOBE FEARON
Pearson Learning Group

Cover design: Marek Antoniak
Cover illustration: William Giese

ISBN: 0-8359-0232-3
Printed in the United Stated of America.

16 17 18   05

Globe
Fearon

Pearson Learning Group

1-800-321-3106
www.pearsonlearning.com

PREFACE

After the English Bible there is probably no background so important to people of our time as the culture of Greece and Rome, with its legends of gods and heroes. Even in this somewhat nonclassical age references to mythological subjects abound. Advertisers, those peerless realists, find many of their allusions among the legends, and some of their brand names. More important, the legends are delightful, charming, worth reading for themselves alone. Yet teachers are increasingly dismayed to find the current crop of students ignorant of even the more famous tales.

For every student who may be familiar with the name of Athena, there are a dozen who have never even heard of her. Artemis, Poseidon, Theseus, Andromache, Achilles, Medea, Persephone—mention of the names brings few gleams of recognition. If knowledge of Greek myths is important to us as the heirs of Western civilization, then we are neglecting our students if we fail to interest them in mythology.

The present edition of the *Odyssey* is an attempt to lure students into "the realms of gold." In my own teaching of the *Odyssey* I have learned many things. I have noticed that the elements in the *Odyssey* that appeal most to young people are those essential to the narrative. The wonders, the monsters, the heroic exploits of Odysseus—these are sure-fire ingredients. The rest are impedimenta.

My own experience has shown that students enjoy most in the *Odyssey:*

1. The narrative; the sweep of a good yarn

PREFACE

2. The marvels and wonders: ingredients of make-believe and fantasy
3. The characterization of Odysseus himself: shrewd, crafty, but human
4. Man encountering seemingly insuperable difficulties; the underdog triumphant

Students enjoy least:

1. Archaic diction and flowery language; difficult vocabulary
2. Long descriptions and Homeric similes
3. Formal elements, such as speeches full of patronymics, stock epithets, and courtly flattery
4. Too many proper names of mystifying spelling and pronunciation

Too often we teachers forget the problems of reading the *Odyssey* for the first time. We forget how difficult the archaic language of many translations can be for young people. In our own more mature interest in Homeric customs and Greek life, we forget that our young people like most the *story*.

The present edition tries to eliminate or minimize the difficulties noted above. It is much more informal in style— almost colloquial at times. And why not? Was not the epic of the *Odyssey* meant for the "common man" of Homer's day? Did it not find its greatest appeal, not among scholars, but among the common folk? As W. H. D. Rouse has said in his remarkable essay, *Homer's Words.* . . .

> "The people who listened to the epic bards . . . knew nothing of books; they were practical men, educated by life, but keenly alive to beauty, and sensitive to fine art. . . ."

PREFACE

Why should the *Odyssey* often seem a wordy, difficult "masterpiece," revered by scholars but disregarded by the people?

The present edition is intended to be read as the wonderful story it is. Without flowering interpolations and courtly repetitions, it is a swift-paced narrative filled with excitement, suspense, and humor. In cutting out some of the leisurely descriptions of Phaeacian customs and old Greek rituals, I have, admittedly, eliminated some excellent material. Perhaps some will regret the loss of many of the Homeric similes and repetitive epithets. But we must always remember how the *Odyssey* looks to a young person of today reading it for the first time.

If we convince the young person that the *Odyssey* is difficult and antiquarian in its appeal, we may lose him for further reading in the delights of mythology. If we get him to enjoy the *Odyssey,* then we have won a convert. Let him come back later to other editions for the full flavor of Greek customs and archaic diction.

The problem of proper names cannot, of course, be eliminated entirely. I have substantially reduced the number included. Supernumeraries and casual bystanders are not, in general, identified by names. To help in keeping straight the *dramatis personae,* a cast of characters follows this preface. Students should be encouraged to use it frequently.

Other supplementary material is included for student use. Since much of the action of the *Odyssey* is mystifying to those who know nothing of the Trojan War, a brief account of that conflict is included on page 223. The more important gods and goddesses are listed on page 259. Objective reading questions based upon each of the chapters begin on page 265.

PREFACE

Enriching Your Reading, page 277, encourages thoughtful discussion of characterization, plot, setting, background, and allied matters.

A useful supplement is the list of suggested activities (page 260). Most of the activities are suitable for normal classes, though study of Tennyson's *Ulysses* is more difficult and might be reserved for superior classes. However, even normal classes can enjoy it with teacher assistance.

This edition of the *Odyssey,* except for two omissions, is reasonably complete as regards the narrative itself. Books I-IV have been eliminated. Students are often confused by the emphasis upon Telemachus in the first four books, and the delayed appearance of Odysseus in Book V. Many teachers begin the *Odyssey* with Book V. Accordingly, this adaptation synopsizes the antecedent action and begins with Calypso's announcement that she will let Odysseus go.

The second omission is slight. The arrival of the suitors in the land of the dead (beginning of Book XXIV) is omitted entirely. Whatever interest the episode adds is lost because to young readers it seems confusing or anticlimactic.

The present edition has attempted to retain the humor of the original, to point it perhaps more than most student editions do. Many students leave the *Odyssey* without realizing they've read anything funny. Two typical examples are these: Odysseus' strategem to get a coat (page 112); his declaration (page 107) that he hates a liar—followed by a whopper of his own.

The difference between this edition and a strictly "literal" translation is apparent from the following insult of Eurymachus (Chapter 14). This is the literal version:

PREFACE

"Hear me, ye suitors of the illustrious queen, while I speak the things which the mind in my breast commands me. This man does not come to the house of Odysseus without the will of some god; to me however the flame of the torches seems to be from him, and his head; since he has no hair; not even a little." (Buckley's literal translation, with *Odysseus* substituted for *Ulysses*.)

The present edition tries to say essentially the same in a more modern idiom:

"Listen, suitors of a noble queen; I have some things to say to you. This beggar probably comes to us through the will of some god. As a matter of fact, the divine fire seems to be shining out of the top of his head, for he has no hair there to stop it."

The freer translation tries to suggest the ribald humor of the suitor, and to draw the setting more completely. Many students reading a more rigorously literal version miss the "wisecrack" completely. I believe the present *Odyssey* is true in spirit to its magnificent original.

I have been interested in the *Odyssey* ever since I read it in Greek with Dr. Edward Chickering many years ago, and later in English with Professor Carleton Brownson. It was then that I first became fascinated by the idea of a good readable version for high school students. In writing this version I have used Buckley's literal translation extensively. I have read various other translations with a great deal of delight, including those by Butcher and Lang, by Bates, by Rieu, and by W. H. D. Rouse.

This has been for me a labor of love. I hope that this book will be a friendly introduction to that master yarn of all,

ix

PREFACE

which puts Superman and his cohorts to shame for sheer imaginative beauty and suspense.

I am indebted to Mr. Thomas Fraumeni for his imaginative drawings scattered throughout the book. The map on the inside cover presented many problems to the artist and to me. The geography of the *Odyssey* is open to many interpretations. Some are familiar; for example, placing Scylla and Charybdis in the Strait of Messina, between Italy and Sicily. Identification of the Ocean Stream with the Atlantic is scarcely surprising. On the other hand, the position of the Clashing Rocks, Aeaea, or Ogygia is open to considerable dispute. We decided finally to take certain liberties with the mythological geography to make a map that would be interesting to students—a map filled with detail and some of the excitement of the *Odyssey*. The lefthand portion, particularly, suggests the mystery and the terror of the unknown, when the sea stretched endlessly to the ends of the world. If the map helps to entice students to read, it will have served part of its purpose. Its other aim is to provide a handy guidebook for the students en route with Odysseus. Students should be urged to make their own simplified copies for classroom use.

I wish to acknowledge my thanks to my very good friend, Mr. Jerome Carlin, Chairman of English at Fort Hamilton High School, Brooklyn, New York, for his thoughtful reading of the manuscript. To my wife Marie E. Christ go my thanks, as ever, for her patient assistance in the production of the finished book.

H. I. C.

TO THE STUDENT

The book you are about to read has been a best seller for 3000 years! In a time when the average best seller is forgotten within a year, that's rather startling news, isn't it? Surely, you'll agree, a book must have *something* to survive for a period more than fifteen times as long as the lifetime of our own country. "But," you're probably thinking, "this is probably a stuffy old story liked and admired only by a few odd graybeards." Not at all!

The *Odyssey* has always been a favorite of young people. Very early in life most children begin to enjoy stories of imagination—tales of giants, fairy princesses, wonderful happenings beyond reality. This love for imaginative stories never quite leaves readers. Even adults enjoy stories of fantasy and make-believe. The *Odyssey* is beloved of all who have active imaginations and a strong love of adventure. This includes most of you who will read this book.

Adventure and excitement mark the *Odyssey*. There is action from beginning to end. Odysseus has to meet monsters, enchantresses, ghosts of the dead, and traitors in his own home. To survive he has to display bravery, cunning, strength, and persistence. He has to face the terrors of the sea with a vessel ill equipped to ride out turbulent Mediterranean storms. You'll find this an exciting tale, indeed.

Before you begin, read the account of the Trojan War on pages 223-228. This will give you the background necessary to understand the *Odyssey* fully. As you read, you'll meet new names. You'll find a helpful list just after this introduc-

TO THE STUDENT

tion. Refer to it whenever you come across a name you've forgotten. Don't be frightened by Greek names. They seem difficult only because they are strange. Probably our own names seem difficult to new immigrants.

Refer frequently to the map on the inside cover. Make a copy for yourself and draw the route of Odysseus' travels as you go along. Chapters 5-8 are most important for this activity. Places are numbered and identified. Do not, of course, write in this book unless you own it.

Suggested activities on page 260, and *Enriching Your Reading*, on page 277, will make the reading of the *Odyssey* more enjoyable. But though you may wish to delve further into mythology and the tales of gods and heroes, read the *Odyssey* first for the story. Don't limit yourself only to a chapter or two at each sitting. If you enjoy it, read on to get the full impact of the narrative. Above all, remember that the *Odyssey* was first composed for enjoyment. This book was designed to give you pleasure, while introducing you to a great story.

IMPORTANT PERSONS AND PLACES

The system of indicating pronunciation has been simplified for student use. Capital letters indicate primary accents; italics indicate secondary accents. Vowel sounds are represented by familiar syllables like ah, ay, *and* ee. *Knowing the accent and the pronunciation of the accented syllable is the clue to the pronunciation of most Greek names. Unstressed vowels in Greek, as in English, tend to sound alike. Page numbers refer to the reader's first acquaintance with the names.*

Achilles (a-KIL-eez), 3 — Greek hero, mightiest fighter at Troy

Aeaea (ee-EE-a), 53 — Circe's island

Aegisthus (ee-JIS-thus), 71 — Helped slay Agamemnon

Aeolia (ee-O-li-a), 49 — Home of god of the winds

Aeolus (EE-o-lus), 49 — God of the winds

Agamemnon (*ag*-a-MEM-non), 25 — Leader of the Greeks against Troy; murdered by his wife Clytemnestra

Agelaus (*a*-je-LAY-us), 183 — One of Penelope's suitors

Ajax (AY-jax), 74 — Greek hero, enemy of Odysseus

Alcinous (al-SIN-o-us), 9 — King of the Phaeacians

Amphinomus (am-FIN-o-mus), 130 — One of Penelope's suitors

Antinous (an-TIN-o-us), 130 — One of Penelope's suitors

Arete (a-REE-tee), 10 — Wife of Alcinous

Argus (AHR-gus), 141 — Odysseus' faithful dog

Artemis (AHR-te-mis), 13 — Goddess of the moon

Athena (a-THEE-na), 7 — Goddess of wisdom, friend to Odysseus

xiii

xiv

TABLE OF CONTENTS

LIST OF ILLUSTRATIONS

FOREWORD

After the Trojan War (be sure to read page 223), the Greek heroes left the shores of Troy for their scattered homelands in Greece. Odysseus, like all the other chieftains, set out cheerfully for Ithaca, far across the sea. The sea! Odysseus' most bitter enemy among the gods was Poseidon, God of the Sea, ruler of the very oceans that Odysseus had to cross. How Poseidon became his enemy and how the god brought about many disasters Odysseus himself will tell. Fortunately, though, Odysseus had a staunch friend among the gods—Athena, goddess of wisdom, powerful daughter of the ruler of the gods, Zeus himself.

At a time when Poseidon was off on a visit to the ends of the earth, Athena seized the opportunity to plead with Zeus on behalf of Odysseus. For after many strange adventures and after the loss of all his men, he had become the unwilling captive of a goddess, Calypso, who loved him. Though longing to return to his home he was powerless against the strength of an immortal. Zeus agreed to help. The god Hermes was sent to tell Calypso to release him, and Calypso had to bow before the will of the most powerful. The tale opens in the tenth year of his wanderings after the fall of Troy. After eight years of captivity Odysseus is surprised to find that Calypso is willing to help him return.

CHAPTER ONE

The Wrath of Poseidon

"Poor Odysseus! Stop worrying. I shall not keep you here any longer. I shall send you away at once if you wish. I want to help you, but you must do your share. Build yourself a good sturdy raft. I'll promise you bread, water, wine, and a strong wind to bear you home again—if the other gods are willing."

As Calypso said this, Odysseus shuddered. "O goddess, you're planning something else when you tell me to cross the wide sea in a raft. Getting across is a difficult job even for swift and sturdy ships. I would not set out in a raft unless you promised to plan no injury against me. For you are a goddess, with strength beyond that of mortals."

"You are wrong," insisted Calypso. "Let heaven and earth be witness that I plan you no harm. I shall take the same care of you that I would take of myself in a similar difficulty. I am not made of iron. I do feel sorry for you. But why do you wish to return home? If you knew how many troubles lie ahead of you before you reach your home, you would prefer to stay here with me—to become an immortal like me. Why do you wish to see your wife again? Surely, she is not more beautiful than I?"

1

"Sacred goddess," diplomatically replied Odysseus, "don't be angry with me. I know that my wife Penelope is inferior to you in all respects. After all, you are immortal and will never be old. But even so, I'd like above all else to return home and to set foot once again on my native soil. If one of the gods again brings me to grief on the sea, I'll have to bear it patiently. I have already suffered much on the sea and in war."

As he spoke, the sun set, and darkness came on. When the dawn had streaked the east with red, Odysseus rose and went to the farthest end of the island where the trees were tallest. With tools that Calypso had supplied, he set about building the raft. He built it wide and strong, with mast, sails, and a rudder. On the fourth day he finished it. On the fifth day immortal Calypso sent him forth well stocked with water and provisions. And she sent him a favorable wind, warm and gentle.

Odysseus spread his sails to the helpful breeze and guided the raft skilfully with the rudder. He kept watch upon the constellations to hold his direction true. He saw the Pleiades, which some call the "Seven Sisters," and the Bear, which others call the "Dipper." Calypso had advised him to keep the Bear on his left so that he would sail toward the east.

For seventeen days he sailed over the sea. On the eighteenth he sighted land, the shadowy mountains of the land of the Phaeacians. But at just this moment Poseidon returned from his far visit. He spied his enemy Odysseus at a distance. Angrily he said to himself, "The moment I turn my back the gods help Odysseus! Still, I will not let him escape scot-free!"

He gathered the clouds, stirred up the sea, and let loose a mighty storm. All the winds struggled at once, sending up towering waves. Odysseus trembled and cried in anguish, "Unlucky Odysseus again! I am afraid that the goddess spoke the truth when she said that I'd have many difficulties before getting back home. My troubles are beginning. In this tempest my destruction seems certain. How lucky were those comrades of mine who died in the Trojan war itself! It would have been better had I been killed the day the Trojans slew great Achilles. At least then I'd have been mourned as a hero. Now I am doomed to die a miserable death."

He had barely finished speaking when a wave sent him ahead, whirling him about at the same time. In the tumult he was swept off the raft, his hands away from the rudder. The mast broke in two, and the sail fell into the sea. He had difficulty in keeping afloat, for his clothes were soaked and heavy. He struggled to the surface, choking on the bitter salt of the sea. Yet he knew enough to try to reach the raft. Barely grasping it he heaved himself on to it once again. The terrible storm continued, tossing the raft about wildly.

In this violent tempest Ino, a lesser goddess of the sea, took pity upon Odysseus. In the midst of the tumult she addressed Odysseus, "Unhappy man, why is Poseidon so angry with you that he plots so many evils for you? Well, have one consolation: he can never destroy you, though he would like to. To save yourself try to reach the land of the Phaeacians. Swim for it! Take this scarf and wind it around your chest. It will protect you from further disaster. But when you reach the shore, throw it back into the sea as far as you can."

Having spoken, the goddess gave him the scarf and disappeared under the waves. Odysseus hesitated a moment. "Alas, perhaps this is more trickery to get me away from the security of the raft. Still I do see land far off in the distance. I'll wait. As long as these planks hold out, I'll stick with the raft. When the raft has been destroyed, then I'll swim. That seems best."

As he was thinking, Poseidon sent another towering wave against him, menacing and terrible. It scattered the planks of the raft like so much chaff in the wind. Odysseus grasped one sturdy plank, and mounted it as if it were a horse. He took off his soggy clothes, put the scarf around his chest, and dove off into the sea, swimming frantically.

Old Poseidon saw him again and muttered, "Good! You are having your troubles now. Even if you do get to shore, you will remember my 'entertainment' for you!" And he drove off in his sea carriage to his magnificent palaces.

The terrible storm continued, tossing the raft about wildly.

Athena took advantage of Poseidon's absence to quiet all the winds except the north wind. She commanded him to help Odysseus reach shore safely once again. Two days Odysseus tossed in the heavy seas. Often he thought death was near. On the third day there was a breathless calm. He could see land near at last. He swam closer and saw to his dismay that the shoreline was rough and jagged with rocks.

Again Odysseus lamented to himself, "My troubles are not over. After struggling to get near the land, I find it surrounded by sharp rocks and smooth cliffs. If I try to land, I may be crushed on a rock. If I swim out again and try to find a better harbor, another storm may cast me back to sea and to my death. I know too well how Poseidon feels about me."

As he pondered, another billow bore him to the rough shore. He would have been crushed and torn to bits if Athena had not warned him to look out. He grasped a rock with both hands and held on until the wave had passed. But the backwash of the wave struck him and carried him out to sea again. The skin on his hands was stripped off. He sank beneath the wave.

Then he would indeed have perished if Athena had not encouraged him again. He swam outside the breakers looking for sloping shores or harbors. At last he came to the mouth of a beautiful flowing river, smooth and sheltered. He prayed aloud to the god of the river, "Hear me, whoever you are. I come to you fleeing the wrath of Poseidon. Take pity on me. I have suffered much already. Even the immortal gods must pity a poor wanderer."

The river god heard, and helped him to the mouth of the river by staying the river's flow. Odysseus sank to his knees, weary and battered by the salt sea. For a moment he lay breathless and speechless, his strength gone. At last he caught his breath and recalled his duty. He took off the scarf that had carried him to safety, and cast it into the river. Then he threw himself down and kissed the earth. Once again he took stock of the situation.

"What shall I suffer next? What will happen to me? If I stay here overnight by the river, the wet, the wind, and the cold will probably be too much for me in my exhausted condition. On the other hand, if I go further inland for protection against the wind, I may make a meal for some beast of prey."

In the end he decided to risk the second course. He hastened to the forest. He found, near the river, a group of trees with a clearing surrounding them. He made a rough bed, heaped leaves over himself, and fell fast asleep.

CHAPTER TWO

The Phaeacian Princess

While Odysseus slept, his faithful friend Athena went into the city of the Phaeacians. Planning the speedy return of Odysseus, she went directly to the house of Alcinous, wise ruler of the land. She hastened to the room that belonged to Nausicaa, beautiful daughter of Alcinous. As a goddess Athena could assume the appearance of any mortal. She appeared to Nausicaa in the form of one of her close friends, and said, "Nausicaa, why are you so careless? You'll be married one of these days. Yet you leave all your beautiful clothing lying about untended. Come, let's go down to wash the linen. I'll help you. After all, you won't be unmarried much longer. Every Phaeacian nobleman would like to wed you. Ask your father to have a wagon and mules ready to carry us in the morning to the distant washing pools."

When she had spoken, Athena went off to Olympus, where people say the gods live. There the winds never blow, nor does it ever rain or snow. There the happy gods spend their carefree days, and there Athena went after speaking to Nausicaa.

In the morning Nausicaa rose and went directly to her father. She found him leaving for a council with the Phaeacians.

"Dear dad, would you prepare a chariot for me, one with good wheels? I must take my clothing to the river for laundering. You know, you ought to have clean linen when you are conferring with your chiefs. Your sons, too, need freshly washed clothes. I have to think about all these things."

She used these excuses because she was too shy to mention her thoughts of marriage. But her father understood and answered, "Take the mules, my child, and anything else you need. Go; the servants will provide you a high cart with a covering over the top."

At his words, the servants went to fulfil his commands. They made ready the mule-cart outside and yoked the mules. Nausicaa placed her best clothing in the cart. Her mother, Arete, prepared a picnic lunch, good food and plenty of it, with some wine in a goatskin. Nausicaa entered, picked up the whip and the reins, and off she went with her attendants.

Soon they reached the river, at a spot ideal for washing. They unyoked the mules and set them to grazing. Having washed the clothes and spread them out to dry, they all bathed and rubbed themselves with olive oil. After their lunch they began to toss a ball around, singing as they played. Nausicaa stood out from the rest both for her beauty and her singing.

As they were about to yoke the mules and return home, Athena decided that Odysseus should awaken. Nausicaa threw the ball to one of the maids, but the girl missed. When the ball fell into the swirling river,

Nausicaa threw the ball to one of the maids.

the girls set up a cry. The shrieks awakened Odysseus. He sat up and thought, What next! What kind of people live here? Are they brutal savages or kindly folk? I wonder if the shrieking I hear is that of mountain nymphs. Perhaps I am near human beings who can understand my language. Well, I'll have to go out to see, I suppose."

So out he crept, covering himself with leaves and twigs. But the girls, when they saw him, fled in terror, for he had been battered by the waves and the sea. Nausicaa alone remained, for Athena gave confidence to her. Odysseus debated what to do. Should he fall on his knees to beg mercy of this strange girl, or should he stand at a distance and politely ask for clothing and directions to the city? He decided to stand his ground and speak mildly to her. He phrased his words diplomatically.

"I ask for mercy, O princess—whether goddess or mortal I cannot tell, for you are like Artemis, daughter of Zeus himself. If you are a mortal, how lucky are your father and mother, and your brothers who must be proud of you! How fortunate the one who becomes your husband—never have I seen a more beautiful woman! I fear to speak to you, but I must.

"I am at the end of my rope. Yesterday, after twenty days of hardship on the stormy sea, I escaped. All that time I was being borne further away from Ogygia. Now fate has cast me ashore here, perhaps to a worse fate. The gods probably still have a few scores to even with me. But, my princess, please pity me. In my misfortune I appeal to you first. I know none other here. Direct me to the city. Give me any old clothing you can spare. May the gods grant you anything you desire—a husband, a house, a happy marriage."

Nausicaa replied, "You do not seem to be either a bad man or a foolish one, but Zeus allots happiness according to his will. You must accept what comes. However, since you have come to our land, you will be given clothing and anything else you need, stranger that you are. I will show you the city, and tell you the name of our people. We are the Phaeacians. I am the daughter of the king, mighty Alcinous."

She turned to her handmaidens and said, "Wait a moment, girls. Why are you flying from the sight of this poor man? Do you think he's an enemy? We have no enemies, for our land is dear to the gods. Besides we are so far from any other shores that no other men have commerce with us. This poor fellow deserves our help, for all strangers are under the protection of Zeus. Give him food and drink."

After Odysseus had washed and rubbed himself with oil, he put on clothing which the girls had provided. Athena made him even more majestic, so that the girls admired him. Then he went off and sat down by the shore, far from the group.

Nausicaa said to the maidens, "Listen a moment. This man comes to us through the will of the gods.

Though he seemed disheveled before, now he seems almost god-like in appearance. He is the kind of person I would like to marry, if he would only stay here. But come, give him something to eat."

Odysseus ate hungrily, for it had been many days since he had eaten. But Nausicaa had other things to think of. She packed the clothing and put it on the cart. Getting into the seat, she encouraged Odysseus, "Come, now, stranger. We're going to the city and to my father's palace. You seem to be a man of good sense. Listen to my plan.

"While we are still out in the countryside, follow close behind the wagon with the girls. I'll lead the way. When we come to the city, though, this plan will not do. For some of the people will say, 'Who is this handsome stranger following Nausicaa? Where did she find him? Is he to be her husband? She rejects all her Phaeacian suitors only to marry a stranger.'

"I don't want any idle gossip that might possibly injure my father and mother. When we come to a beautiful grove, wait there until you think we have reached the city. Then go to the city and ask for my father, Alcinous. Anyone will direct you to my father's house. When you get inside, go directly to my mother. Throw yourself upon her mercy, asking for help on your homeward journey. If she is pleased with you, there's a good chance that you will again see your friends, your house, and your native land."

She whipped up the mules and drove off quickly. At sunset they came to the grove. The girls went on, but Odysseus sat down and prayed to Athena, "Help me, O goddess, so that the Phaeacians will pity me and aid me."

Athena heard his prayer, but did not appear to him. For she feared the wrath of Poseidon, who was still angry with Odysseus.

CHAPTER THREE

In The Palace of The King

While Odysseus prayed, the wagon carried Nausicaa to the city. When Odysseus judged that she had arrived, he set out for the city himself. Athena enveloped him in a mist so that he would not be challenged by any of the Phaeacians. Near the city Athena took on the likeness of a young woman and stood before him. Odysseus spoke to her.

"Child, can you direct me to the house of Alcinous, the ruler of this land? I am a stranger from a distant land and know no one here."

"I can help you. My own father lives near him. Follow me in silence. Do not speak to any of the men, for they do not like strangers. We are far from the lands of any other men and trust in our swift ships for our safety."

Having spoken, Athena led the way. Again she surrounded him with a mist, so that no one saw him, though his own vision was clear and he was amazed at their buildings. At the palace gates Athena again spoke.

"This is the house you asked me to show you. Alcinous is dining. Go right in. Don't be afraid. The bold man succeeds in everything. Go right up to the queen,

Arete. She has good sense. If she likes you, you may still see your home again."

After Athena left, Odysseus went into the magnificent palace of Alcinous, admiring everything as he went. He saw the leaders of the Phaeacians feasting, but he went straight on until he came to Queen Arete and King Alcinous. He threw himself at the feet of the queen and declared, "O Arete, I come to you after many hardships to ask for an escort so that I may reach my native land. I have been away many years and long to see my friends once more."

Having spoken he sat down upon the hearth in the ashes, but the others were speechless with amazement. At last an aged hero, who knew the old traditions, addressed his king.

"O Alcinous, it is not right to let a stranger among us sit in the dust of the hearth. Come, take the stranger by the hand and lead him to a seat of honor. Give him food and drink, for one should not disregard a stranger's requests."

Alcinous followed the suggestion, giving Odysseus a seat of honor next to himself. After Odysseus had taken food and wine, Alcinous spoke to his men.

"Listen a moment, leaders and rulers of the Phaeacians. Now that you have finished your feasting, go home to rest. In the morning we shall call a fuller meeting of the elders. We shall entertain the stranger and offer suitable sacrifices. Afterward we shall send the stranger quickly to his own home with an escort,

He threw himself at the feet of the queen.

although he is still far away from home. We shall see to it that he suffers no misfortunes on the way home, but after he reaches home he will have to suffer whatever his fate may be.

"If he is one of the immortals from heaven, then the gods are playing us a new trick, for in the past they have always shown themselves to us undisguised."

Odysseus answered openly, "Do not concern yourself with that possibility, Alcinous. I am not like a god either in person or in appearance. I am like mankind, particularly those men who have known grief and toil. I could tell you many misfortunes that have come to me by the will of the gods. But, please, as soon as morning comes, help me, unfortunate that I am, to reach my own country. I'd give my life to see my home, my servants, and my native land."

All the company approved the stranger's words. After they had drunk their last drops, they went home, leaving Odysseus beside Arete and Alcinous. As the handmaidens were taking away the dishes, clever Arete recognized the clothing that Odysseus was wearing. She herself had helped to make the garments! She spoke pointedly, "Stranger, I'll ask you the first questions. Who are you? From where did you come? Who gave you these clothes? Didn't you just say that you had been drifting helpless across the seas?"

Odysseus answered promptly, "It is difficult to tell all my troubles, for the gods have given me many.

However, this much I can say easily. Far off in the sea there lies an island, Ogygia. There lives a deceitful goddess Calypso, beautiful but terrible. No one ever visits her. As luck would have it, I wandered into her clutches after Zeus had sunk my ship on the dark sea. All my companions were drowned, but I survived by lying across the ship's keel. For nine days I floated. On the tenth the gods had me reach Ogygia, where Calypso lives.

"She fell in love with me, took care of me, and vowed she would make me immortal. I was not convinced. I remained there tearfully for seven years. In the eighth year she allowed me to go, declaring that Zeus had commanded my release. Perhaps she had changed her mind. At any rate she gave me a raft and provisions, provided a helpful wind, and sent me on.

"I sailed for seventeen days. On the eighteenth the mountains of your own land appeared. I rejoiced, foolish one, for no sooner had I done so than Poseidon worked his will upon me. He roused up the winds, stirred the sea, and wrecked the raft. I swam for land as best I could. Just as I neared shore a powerful wave dashed me on the rocks. I escaped narrowly and swam out to sea again. Soon I came to the mouth of the river. This seemed smooth and sheltered. I made land, slept among the thickets, and was awakened by the shrieks of your daughter's maids. Among them she seemed like a goddess.

"I begged her assistance. She proved to have good

sense beyond her years. She provided me food, drink and clothing, and here I am. That is the true story of an unfortunate man."

"I must say," declared Alcinous, "that I think my daughter did not show such good sense after all. She should have brought you home with the maids. After all, you asked her assistance first."

Odysseus had a quick answer.

"My lord, don't scold your daughter. She did ask me to follow, but I hesitated to do so, fearing I might anger you."

Alcinous answered, "My friend, I am not one to insist upon trifles. It is better to do things properly. However, you impress me as the kind of man I'd like for a son-in-law. If you would remain willingly, I'd give you house and possessions. But no one here will keep you against your will. I shall make ready your voyage tomorrow; don't worry. Sleep until then. My men will take you home, no matter where you live. You will see how wonderful my men and my ships are."

Odysseus was very happy to hear this promise. He prayed aloud and said, "O father Zeus, may Alcinous do everything he has pledged. Then may his praises be sung all over the earth."

While they were speaking, Arete ordered her servants to prepare the bed for Odysseus. When they had finished, they came to Odysseus and said, "Sir, your bed is made." And so Odysseus slept soundly after all his troubles.

CHAPTER FOUR

Phaeacian Sports

At daybreak both Alcinous and Odysseus rose. Alcinous led the way to a place by the ships where the meeting was to be held. Athena took the form of the king's herald and mingled with the crowds, saying, "Come, leaders and chieftains, to the assembly to hear about the stranger who came over the wide sea. He is a man who seems like a visitor from the gods."

Thus she incited their curiosity. Seats were quickly filled. Many admired Odysseus when they saw him, for Athena had added majesty to his appearance. She made him taller and more powerful. The Phaeacians were impressed. When they had all come together, Alcinous began to speak.

"Captains and counselors, I ask your attention. This stranger—I don't know who he is—has come wandering into my house. He has asked for an escort to his own land, which according to our custom we must provide. We shall choose fifty-two of the best oarsmen among you. When you have prepared the ships, come into the palace for a feast. So much for you young people." And he turned to the elders.

"You, my lords, come to my house at once. We shall entertain our visitor in good style. I will not take *no* for an answer. Call the minstrel Demodocus, for there is no one like him about to raise our spirits in song."

Alcinous led the way, and all the princes followed, except the herald who went for Demodocus. The young men who had been chosen as oarsmen prepared the ships and then went to the palace. There all the Phaeacians gathered, young and old alike.

Soon the herald came with Demodocus, who had lost the sight of his eyes but who had retained the power of song. He led Demodocus to a place of honor, and then the feasting began.

When the guests had had enough to eat, the minstrel began to sing the stories of famous men. He sang of a famous quarrel, the dispute between Achilles and Odysseus at the beginning of the Trojan War. He told how Agamemnon, leader of the Greeks against Troy, had rejoiced at the quarrel because of a prophecy that Troy would not be taken before two Greek leaders quarreled. Little did Agamemnon know that his own later quarrel with Achilles was the dispute referred to.

At the recital of all these familiar tales Odysseus drew the robe over his face so that the company would not see the tears in his eyes. But Alcinous, sitting near him, noticed his weeping. He spoke at once to his men, "Enough of the banquet and song. Now let us begin the day's contests, so that the stranger may tell his people how able the Phaeacians are in all sports."

At the suggestion the company disbanded and reassembled at the outdoor meeting-place. A great crowd of powerful young men was there, champions in every field of sports. Euryalus and Laodamas were two of the mighty heroes. Running, wrestling, hurdling, jumping, weight-throwing, and boxing were some of the contests held.

After the contests Laodamas, son of Alcinous, addressed the others. "Come, friends, let's ask the stranger if he is skilled in any sport. He is powerfully built, but it is plain that misfortune has somewhat weakened him. The sea is a great sapper of strength."

Euryalus agreed. "A good suggestion, Laodamas. Speak to him."

Accordingly Laodamas went to Odysseus and said, "Come, stranger, join the games, if you feel competent to take part. Forget your cares. It won't take long. The ship is nearly ready for you."

Odysseus replied, "Laodamas, why do you say such things and make sport of me? I am thinking more of my troubles than of games. I've had suffering and sorrow aplenty. All I ask is a safe return."

But Euryalus led him on, saying, "Oh well, I am not classifying you as a person who thinks of nothing but games. You look more like a merchant than a sportsman anyway."

Odysseus, his anger aroused, answered, "I don't care for your way of speaking. Not every man can be as fortunately endowed as you. A man may be weak in physical accomplishments but strong in others. Some look like gods and speak like fools. You have annoyed me by your uncomplimentary remarks. I am not as clumsy as you seem to think; I was a first-rate athlete in my youth. Now, though, wars and calamities have been my lot, and shipwrecks besides. Still, though I have suffered much, I'll take part, for your speech has irritated me, and your words have provoked me."

He sprang up, forgetting his cloak, and seized a weight far heavier than those the other champions had used. Whirling it around his head, he hurled it powerfully. The stone whizzed through the air and the Phaeacians ducked. It flew far above all the previous marks made by the others.

Athena, this time in the likeness of a referee, cried out, "Even a blind man could find your mark, stranger, for it's far ahead of all the others. This contest is yours. No one here can beat that toss!"

Odysseus was happy to find a friend among the strangers. He turned to the Phaeacians and declared gaily, "Try to beat this, my friends. If you do, I'll throw another even larger. Is there anyone else who would like to try the contest—in boxing, wrestling, running? I admit it—you have annoyed me. I'll take on any comers except my host. I can use the bow and arrow. I can throw a javelin as far as anyone else can shoot an arrow. In running, I confess I'll probably do poorly, for I have been aboard ship a long time."

After he spoke, the rest were silent. At last Alcinous spoke up.

"My friend, we find no fault with what you have said. After all, you merely wish to defend yourself after the taunting this fellow gave you. No sensible person would scorn your ability. Listen a moment so that you will take home with you a pleasant memory of our skills. True, we are not the best wrestlers or boxers, but we are good runners and first-rate seamen. We like feasting, singing, music, dancing, and clean linen. Come, dancers, perform for our friend. Let him tell his friends how we excel in sailing, running, dancing, and singing. Get the harp for Demodocus. It's at hand somewhere."

After he spoke, the herald fetched the harp for Demodocus. The blind minstrel went into the center, and the Phaeacians surrounded him. Then began the dance. Odysseus was much impressed with their grace and rhythm.

"O King Alcinous, you declared that your people are superlative dancers. You were right. Their dancing skill amazes me."

Alcinous was delighted at the compliment and turned to his people. "Did you hear that, my lords and princes? The stranger shows good sense. Let us make him a present of clothing and of gold. Let all contribute to the gift. And Euryalus ought to apologize and present a gift, too, for he spoke rather rudely."

The princes applauded and sent messengers for gifts. Euryalus turned to the king and said, "Certainly I shall make amends to the stranger as you suggest. I present him with this sword of bronze and silver, with

Whirling it around his head, he hurled it powerfully.

its scabbard of ivory. This will make amends for my words."

With that he placed the silver-studded sword in Odysseus' hands and said courteously, "My respects to you, sir. If I have spoken unwisely, may the winds carry off the words. My wish to you is this: may the gods allow you to see your wife and your native land again. You have suffered a long time away from your friends."

Odysseus replied, "I wish you well, too, my friend. May the gods grant you happiness. I hope you never regret having given me this beautiful weapon."

As he spoke, he put on the silver-studded sword. All the other gifts were brought in just as the sun was setting. They were placed near Arete. Alcinous turned to his wife and said, "My dear, bring out the best chest we have, and put into it some new clothing. Let the stranger see all the gifts that the Phaeacians have gathered. For my part, I am presenting him with this beautiful golden cup as a remembrance all his days."

Then all went out of the hall into the banquet room. On the way Odysseus saw Nausicaa standing by a pillar. She looked at him admiringly and said at last, "Goodbye, stranger, and a good voyage. When you reach your native land, think of me once in a while, for it is to me, before all others, that you owe your life."

"Princess Nausicaa," replied Odysseus thoughtfully, "if Zeus will grant me a safe voyage home, I shall pray to you, as a goddess, all my days. For you did, indeed, save my life."

Then Odysseus mounted a throne near Alcinous, and all the guests began their banquet. After all had eaten their fill, Odysseus turned to the blind minstrel Demodocus and said, "My friend, your ballads about the heroes of old have been stirring and wonderful to hear. I wish now that you'd tell a different tale. Sing of the Trojan War, particularly of the making of the Wooden Horse, which finally brought about the downfall of Troy. Tell how the Greeks, through the schemes of Odysseus, finally brought the horse into the city itself. If you can tell this story well, then I'll declare before everybody that you are indeed divinely inspired."

Demodocus, having asked the gods for inspiration, answered Odysseus' request and began the story of the Trojan Horse. In ballad form he told how the Greeks pretended to sail away from Troy after ten long years of besieging it in vain, and how they left behind the huge, hollow horse. He described the trick by which the Trojans were persuaded to take the Horse into the city, although it was filled with armed men led by the hero Odysseus. He told how the Greeks poured forth, in the dead of night, to destroy the city. He praised the deeds of Odysseus, who was responsible for the stratagem and who distinguished himself in the fighting.

As the minstrel sang his ballads, Odysseus was reminded of all his troubles and wept bitterly. Once again, only Alcinous noticed his weeping. He interrupted the song at once. "One moment, my princes. Demodocus, please stop your singing. These songs are not pleasant to all of us here. Since you began, our guest has been weeping bitterly. If you stop, we can all once again be merry.

"And you, my good sir, please do not be so secretive about your past. Tell us your name, your birthplace, and the place you now live in, so that our escort may get you there. . . . Tell us about your wanderings, what places you have seen, what men you have met. Tell us which men are friendly and just. Tell us which are cruel and unjust. Judging by your weeping at the song of Troy, you have lost someone dear to you in that terrible war—perhaps a close relative. Am I right? Perhaps you lost a close friend—one as dear to you as a brother?"

CHAPTER FIVE

The One-Eyed Giant

"King Alcinous," replied Odysseus," I really enjoyed listening to your wonderful singer. But you have asked about my troubles. I am afraid that merely thinking about them gives me more sorrow. How can I tell you all of them? Where can I begin? Well, first of all I'll tell you my name. I am Odysseus, son of Laertes, famed throughout the entire world. My home is Ithaca, one of the islands off the coast of Greece. It is rugged country, but a wonderful place just the same. Both Calypso and that other witch Circe kept me practically a prisoner, hoping that I would stay with them. But they never made me forget my home, for there is nothing sweeter than a man's own coun try. If you like, I'll tell you about my attempt to return home from Troy."

And this is the story Odysseus told.

* * *

We had a good start. A favorable wind took us from Troy to the land of the Ciconians in Ismarus. Needing provisions we destroyed the city and killed all the men. We divided the spoil from the city, each one getting an equal share. I suggested that we leave at once, but the others were foolish and decided to stay on. They drank heavily and killed many sheep and

34

cattle for a feast. In the meantime, though, word got through to a neighboring tribe of the Ciconians. These neighbors were much better fighters, skilled on horse as well as on foot.

They attacked us in the morning, in a horde as numerous as leaves in spring. Matters went badly for us. They formed ranks near the ships and raked us with volleys from both sides. We fought them off as best we could, though we were far outnumbered. By evening they had us in full retreat. We lost six men from each ship, but the rest of us fortunately escaped. We set sail at once, grieving at the loss of our comrades, but rejoicing at our own good luck.

After we were at sea a short time, Zeus stirred up a frightening storm. The clouds blanketed the sky, and night set in too early. Our sails were torn in so many places we let them down so that we'd not be completely lost. For two days and two nights there was no let-up. On the morning of the third day the clouds scattered, and we drew up the sails again. We set our course and hoped for the best. I probably would have made my home without incident if a powerful north wind had not swept us off our course. Just as we were rounding the dangerous straits of Malea, off the coast of southern Greece, the north wind blew us off to the southwestward. The villainous wind took me in the wrong direction for nine days.

The tenth day brought us to the land of the Lotus-Eaters. These people eat flowers for food. We disembarked, replenished our water supply, and ate our supper on the shore. After we had eaten, I sent three of my companions as messengers to find out what kind of people these were—these flower-eaters.

The messengers went among the natives. Innocently enough, the Lotus-Eaters offered lotus for my comrades to taste. When my men ate of the flowers, they forgot everything that had happened to them. They no longer wanted to return home, but wished to stay on there, eating the lotus in forgetfulness. I had to drag them off by force and bind them in the ships. I urged my other comrades to sail immediately, for I dreaded what would happen if more men tasted the lotus. We set out promptly, rowing steadily away from land.

We were in low spirits at our bad luck thus far. But we hadn't an inkling of what was in store for us. We reached next the land of the Cyclopes. These monsters are savages without laws or culture. They live by themselves. Each family is a law unto itself. No man cares for his neighbor.

Across their harbor there lies a beautiful wooded island. Wild goats are plentiful there, for there are no hunters to kill them. The Cyclopes just don't have the ships to reach the island, and so it is neglected. It is a rich, fertile place, with drinking water in abundance. A wonderful island! We were fortunate to reach it through a night that made everything invisible. We lay down on the shore, not knowing where we were.

In the morning we awoke and were amazed at our good fortune. We explored the island and found the goats in abundance. We killed a great number of them. As a matter of fact, each of my twelve ships was allotted nine goats. We feasted all day long, adding to our meal the wine we had plundered from the Ciconians.

My curiosity was aroused, unfortunately, at the sight of the mainland. We could see the smoke and hear the voices of the Cyclopes. The next day I addressed my men, having called them all together for a meeting.

"My beloved companions, please wait for me here. I am taking one ship over to the mainland. I'd like to find out what kind of people these Cyclopes are. I'd like to know whether they are insolent, cruel, and unjust, or kindly and hospitable."

I set out, with my men, for the mainland. When we neared land, we saw a lonely cave in which cattle, sheep and goats were housed. There lived a giant, evidently an outcast even from his own people. His name, as I learned later, was Polyphemus. He was really a monster, not like a man at all but like a mountain! He had but one round eye in the middle of his forehead. I ordered my men to stay there near the ship. I chose twelve of my best comrades and went to investigate. I took with me a goatskin of dark wine, which had

been given me by a priest of Apollo. I brought some
provisions, too, for I had a feeling that we were about
to meet a man powerful and savage.

When we reached the cave, we found it empty. The
Cyclops was out pasturing his fat flocks. We looked
at everything with interest. Food there was in abundance! There were baskets filled with cheeses. Pans
were swimming with milk and cream. Lambs and kids
were separated according to their size. My men urged
me to take some of the cheeses, lead the animals into
the ships, and be off. I didn't listen to them. If I only
had! I wanted to meet the Cyclops and receive the
stranger's gifts from him. As it happened, his gifts
were far from pleasant to me or my companions.

We lit a fire and waited, eating of his cheeses. He
came in with a great bundle of dry wood for the fire
and threw it down with a great shout. We were terrified and hid in the back of the cave. He drove the animals into the cave for milking, and closed off the entrance with a huge rock. After he had milked the
animals, he spied us.

"Who are you?" he cried out. "What place did you
come from? Are you merchants, or sea-robbers ready
to kill and be killed for gain?"

We trembled at his words, for we feared him. His
monstrous size and heavy voice were no comfort to
us. Yet I had to answer him; so I said, "We are Greeks
on our way home from Troy. We have been driven far
out of our course by wind and storm. We are proud to

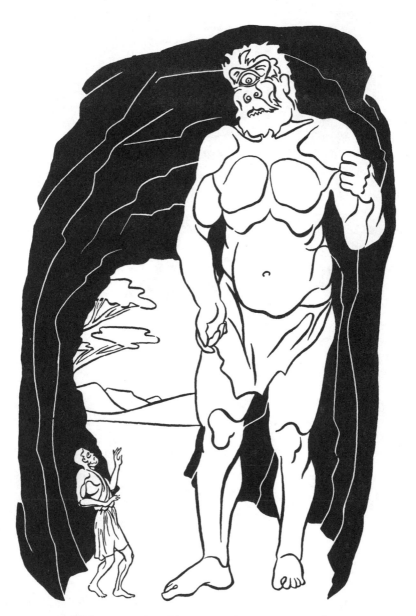

We trembled at his words, for we feared him.

be followers of Agamemnon, leader of all the Greeks against Troy. His fame has spread to all corners of the earth. We are here to make a request of you. We ask hospitable treatment and such gifts as are due to strangers. Honor the gods, O noble sir, and treat us well. For Zeus protects strangers and those who need help."

He answered cruelly, "You're a fool, my friend, to think that I would fear the gods. We Cyclopes have no respect for any of the 'blessed' gods. We are much above them. If I wish to lay hands upon you or your companions, Zeus won't stop me. But tell me where you keep your ship. Near here? Let me know."

He thought he could trick me into revealing the hiding place of the ship. But I gave him a deceitful answer.

"Poseidon the Earth-Shaker wrecked my ship against the rocks of your island. These men with me are all that escaped destruction."

He didn't bother to answer. Instead he rushed forward and grasped two of my companions. Snatching them like puppies he dashed them against the ground, crushing their skulls. Their brains oozed out on the earth. Cutting them up, limb by limb, he prepared his supper. He devoured them like a mountain lion, leaving no trace of the poor men.

We wept aloud, raised our hands heavenward and prayed for Zeus' assistance. We were without hope. After the Cyclops had eaten, he lay stretched out in the cave and slept. I drew my sword and approached him, thinking to kill him or at least wound him seriously. I stopped. How would I get out? We could never have moved the stone from the cavern's opening. Despondently we waited for morning.

The Cyclops awoke after many hours. He went about his business systematically, milking his cattle and performing other chores. After he finished, he snatched two more of my men and prepared his meal. He ate them and then proceeded to drive the cattle from the cage. When the last had gone through, he again rolled the stone in front of the cave's mouth.

I considered many plans for getting revenge if Athena would only grant my prayer. One plan seemed to be best. There was a huge club in the cave, which the Cyclops had been preparing as a walking stick. It was as big as the mast of a good-sized ship. I cut off a piece about six feet long and had my companions sharpen it. I charred the end and brought it to a good point. I asked the men to draw lots to see who would have the job, with me, of thrusting the stick into the eye of the sleeping Cyclops. Four good men were chosen.

In the evening he again herded his fine cattle and sheep into the cave. He put his barrier back into place and milked the animals. Again, after his chores were finished, he snatched two men and prepared his supper. I went close to the Cyclops and said, "Here, Cyclops, have a drink of wine after your meal of human flesh. I want you to know what kind of drink we had aboard my ship. I brought it originally as a gift offering, so that you would pity me and help me return home. Now I see you are mad beyond all cure. How can you expect men to visit you? You have behaved so cruelly."

He took the wine and gulped it down. Licking his lips he spoke again.

"Some more, please, and tell me your name. I'd like to give you a present that you'll approve. Our wine is good, but this is fit for the gods."

I gave him another draught, and he drank it quickly. Again I offered, and again he drank the wine. At last, when he began to feel the effect of the wine, I said gently, "Cyclops, did you ask my name? Well then, I'll tell you, but don't forget that gift you promised me. No-man is my name. My mother, my father, and all my companions call me No-man."

"No-man," he replied with a cruel grin, "this is my present to you. I'll eat all your companions first. I'll save you till last!"

As he said this, he lurched over and fell upon his back. Sleep overcame him. He became ill in his drunken stupor and vomited wine and bits of human flesh. I put the olive-wood stick in the ashes until it was warm. I kept encouraging my companions to keep their spirits high.

The stick was green; when it was about to take fire, green though it was, I took it out and approached the one-eyed monster. My companions hesitated a moment, but some god inspired them with courage. They took hold of the stake and thrust the point into his eye. I leaned on it from above and turned it round and round, as a man drills a hole. Taking the white-hot stake we twisted it in his eye, and the hot blood flowed around it. We scorched his eyebrows and eyelids as the eyeball burned with a hissing sound.

The Cyclops howled horribly and we drew away in terror. He drew the stake from his eye and threw it with an anguished cry from his hands. He called aloud to the other Cyclopes who lived around him in caves. They heard him and came to find out what was the matter. They stood around the cave and cried out his name.

"What terrible injury, Polyphemus, has made you cry out so in the middle of the night? Is some man driving away your sheep against your will? Is someone killing you by force or by trickery?"

"O my friends," answered mighty Polyphemus, "No-man is killing me, by trickery and not by force."

"Well then," they said, "if no man is assaulting you, you must be sick, and sickness is heaven sent. You'd better pray to your father, the great god Poseidon."

They left. I laughed inwardly because my name and strategem had worked. But the Cyclops, groaning and weeping from pain, rolled away the stone from the opening. Taking no chances, he sat within the gate and stretched forth his hands. As his flocks went out to graze, he felt each sheep to make certain that none of us tried to escape this way. He must have taken me for a fool! I had been casting about for some plan to save my companions and me, for the future still looked very dark. At last I hit upon this trick.

The rams were sturdy and large, with rich dark coats. I tied them in threes, putting one of my companions under each middle ram. Thus three sheep carried one man. I chose a different method for myself. I picked out the biggest and heaviest ram. I laid hold of its back and slung myself under its shaggy belly. I hung upside down, holding on to the wonderful wool. Thus we awaited the morning.

At dawn the animals rushed to the pasture. The Cyclops, still suffering greatly, felt the backs of all the sheep as they went out. The fool did not realize that my men were tied underneath the sheep. My own sturdy ram went out last, weighed down by his heavy coat and by me. Putting his hand on the ram's back, Polyphemus said, "Dear ram, why are you the last out today? You are not usually the last. You're usually first out and first back. Now you're way behind. Do you feel sorry for the loss of my eye, which a foul villain has blinded after first making me drunk? Well, No-man has not yet escaped. If you could only speak and tell me where he's hiding, I'd dash his brains out on the spot. Then and then only would I rest again."

At his last words he sent the ram away from him

out of the cave. A little further on I dropped from the ram and freed my companions. We quickly drove his cattle on until we came to our ship. We who had narrowly escaped death were a welcome sight to the companions we had left aboard ship, but they began to weep for the men who had died. I gave them little time for weeping, for I ordered them to be off at once. When we were a good distance from the mainland, I couldn't resist a parting insult to Polyphemus.

"Hello there, Cyclops, you thought you had a weakling there in the cave when you murdered my companions. Your sins came home to roost, you monster. Since you didn't hesitate to eat your guests, the gods have had revenge upon you."

He was furious. He tore off the top of a large mountain and threw it in the direction of the voice. The missile landed in front of our boat and drove it back toward shore! I took a long pole and pushed powerfully, meanwhile urging my comrades to row with all their might. Soon we were twice as far away as before. I started to shout again.

My comrades tried to stop me. "Foolish man, why do you try to irritate a fierce monster? Just a moment ago he threw a huge rock into the sea and nearly brought us back to shore and our deaths. If he had heard any of us speaking, he'd have crushed us with a rock. He throws far enough."

I was too stubborn to listen. I spoke up again in my anger.

"O Cyclops, if anybody asks about that unsightly eye you have there, just say that Odysseus, destroyer of cities, son of Laertes, blinded you!"

He answered with a wail. "Alas, the old prophecies are coming true. They said I'd lose my sight through the trickery of Odysseus. I have always been expecting a strong, handsome man. Instead a puny weakling has blinded me after conquering me with wine. Come back, Odysseus, so that I can give you suitable presents. I shall urge my father, illustrious Poseidon, god of the sea, to get you back home safely. He will cure my loss of sight, if he chooses, without the help of any other gods."

"I wish I could kill you," I replied, "and send you to Hades where no one could ever cure you—not even Poseidon."

He stretched forth his hands and prayed aloud.

"Hear me, father Poseidon, see to it that Odysseus, destroyer of cities, never reaches his home. If you can't quite do that, if it is his fate to get there eventually, delay him and destroy all his companions. Arrange matters so that he finds great troubles at home."

So he prayed and his father heard him. But Polyphemus raised a much larger stone and sent it flying. This time it just missed the rudder, landing behind the ship. The sea surged up around us as the rock fell. The waves sent us forward to the little island. There we found the other ships and the rest of our comrades. They had almost given up hope, but were glad to see us. We divided the Cyclops' animals evenly. I sacrificed the ram to Zeus, but he did not listen. For as it turned out he had planned the destruction of all my ships and all my men.

We feasted throughout the whole day, and slept that night by the shore of the sea. In the morning we embarked on our ships, rejoicing at our narrow escapes and grieving at our losses.

CHAPTER SIX

The Sorceress

Soon we reached the floating island of Aeolia, where Aeolus, God of the Winds, lives. He entertained me for a whole month and asked many questions about Troy and the return of the Greeks. I satisfied his curiosity as best I could. When at last I spoke of leaving and asked for his help, he agreed. He gave me the skin of an ox, which he made into a bag. He bound all the raging winds and trapped them in the bag. He freed only the west wind to help us on our voyage home. A good idea, but our own stupidity spoiled it!

We sailed splendidly for nine days. On the tenth we saw at last the island of our homeland. We could even see men on shore—tending their fires. Happy but exhausted I fell asleep. While I slept, the men spoke to each other, declaring that I was taking home gold and silver, presents from Aeolus.

One of the men said, "What a lucky man this Odysseus is! He comes home wealthy from Troy, but the rest of us, comrades on that long journey, come home empty handed. Out of friendship Aeolus has given him all the gold and silver that bag can hold. Hurry, let's see what he has there."

The evil suggestion took hold. The men untied the bag, and all the winds rushed out. The storms bore them far away from home, me with them. When I awoke, I debated whether I ought to perish in the sea and be done with it, or still continue the attempt to get home. I decided to fight it out.

The winds carried us back to Aeolia. There we went ashore and took on water. My companions ate near the ships. With a companion I went again to the house of Aeolus. I found him at a banquet.

"Why are you back here, Odysseus?" he asked. "Surely we sent you away fully provided for the homeward journey."

"Evil companions are responsible," I replied, "and sleep. But help me again, dear friends, for you have the power."

Thus I tried to soothe them with gentle words, but no one answered. At last Aeolus said, "Get away from here at once, foul man. I do not wish to have anything to do with a person who is cursed by the gods. Away at once."

I left with a heavy heart. We sailed off, grieving at our misfortune. This time we had no help from the winds. We sailed for six days. On the seventh we came to a city of Lamos called Laestrygonia. We entered a fine harbor. Inside the harbor two headlands projected, forming a quiet pool ideal for ships. All the other ships sailed into this narrow haven. Through some good fortune, I decided not to enter this inner harbor but kept my ship outside.

I climbed a rugged peak to get a view. Smoke was

The men untied the bag, and all the winds rushed out.

rising off in the distance. I sent some messengers to inquire about the people. They went ashore and were directed to the king's palace. Inside they found the king's wife, a giantess as big as the peak of a mountain. Her husband arrived soon after, another monster. He snatched one of my men and prepared his supper. The other two escaped, but the monster set up a cry.

Out came the strong Laestrygonians, giants, not men. They threw heavy stones at the ships trapped in the narrow harbor. Cries arose from the stricken ships as the men were thrown into the water. The giants stuck the men like fish and carried them off for their feast. While the horrible spectacle was going on in the inner haven, I cut the cables of my ship and urged my comrades to exert themselves in rowing. Our one ship escaped. All the others were destroyed —with all the men.

We sailed on from that place, rejoicing at our own good luck but miserable over the loss of our friends. Next we reached the island of Aeaea, home of the goddess Circe. We disembarked there and lay grief-stricken for two days.

On the third day I meant to have a look around. I went to a lookout for signs of human habitation. Off in the distance I could see smoke—as it turned out, from the palace of Circe. I debated whether I ought to go first. On second thought I decided to care for my men and to send scouts on ahead. As luck would

have it I came upon a huge stag coming down to drink.
I struck him, and the spear passed right through him.
I went back to the ship, carrying the stag across my
back. I threw it down in front of the ship and cheered
my men.

"Come, my friends, we're not lost yet. We certainly
won't starve to death."

Their spirits revived when they saw the magnificent
stag. They prepared a glorious banquet, and we
feasted the whole day. In the morning I called them
together and addressed them.

"My friends, east and west mean nothing to us
here. I don't know what to do. We're on an island in
the middle of the sea. There's no other land in sight,
but I did see smoke off in the distance. Any sugges-
tions?"

When I said this, they shivered in terror, for they
remembered the deeds of Laestrygonian cannibals
and the giant Cyclops. They wept bitterly—much good
that did!

I divided our group into two parties, each with a
leader. I commanded one party, and Eurylochus led the
other. We shook lots in a helmet, and the lot of Eurylochus fell out. He prepared to go, though he and his
companions wept. They were nervous, for they knew
not what lay ahead of them. At last they set off.

High on a hilltop in the woods they found the house
of Circe. All around were fierce wolves and lions
which she had tamed. They did not attack the men,

but wagged their tails as friendlily as you please. The men heard the goddess Circe singing with a beautiful voice. One of them spoke to his comrades.

"Friends, someone inside is singing beautifully. Let's go in, whether she's a goddess or a woman, and speak to her."

They shouted to her, and she came out at once. When she asked them to come in, they followed her innocently. Only Eurylochus stayed outside, fearing some trick. She led them in and invited them to be seated. Then she prepared a meal of cheese and honey, but she mixed magic drugs with the food. When they had eaten, she struck them with a rod and herded them into the pigsty. For they now had pigs' heads, grunts, and bristles. Indeed, she had changed them wholly into swine, but their minds were the minds of men. They wept aloud as she penned them up. She threw them beechnuts and acorns, the kind that pigs like to eat.

Eurylochus came back at once to tell us the news of the sorcery. He could scarcely speak, so grief-stricken was he. But we were so amazed at his behavior that he finally spoke to us.

"We went through the woods as you commanded, Odysseus, until we came to the source of the smoke. We found a beautiful house on a hill. Inside some goddess or woman was singing in a beautiful voice. Our comrades shouted. She came out, called to them, and led them inside. They all followed innocently enough, but I stayed out, fearing a trap. They all vanished. I waited and waited, but no one came out. That's the last I saw of them."

I put on my sword, picked up my bow, and asked him to show me the way to the house. He fell to his knees and begged that I would not send him back.

"Please don't take me there against my will, but leave me here. I am sure that you'll never come back, nor will you bring back any of our comrades. Let's set sail at once. We may yet escape."

"Very well, Eurylochus," I replied, "stay here and wait. I'm going."

I set off for the house at once. When I got near the house of Circe, who should meet me but Hermes, god of the golden wand! He was in the form of a young man. He took me by the hand and said, "Poor fool, where are you going, alone in a country you know nothing about? Are you going to free your companions, who have been enchanted by Circe? That is what you think! You will be trapped there just as the others were. I am willing to help you. Take this powerful drug. It will help you to ward off the magic tricks of Circe.

"She will prepare a magic mixture for you, but the drug will keep you from falling under the spell. When she strikes you with her wand, then draw your sword quickly and rush toward her as if to kill her. Crouching in fear, she will ask for mercy. Make her swear an oath that she will plan no further evil for you or your companions."

Hermes gave me the magic root and explained its power. Then he went off to high Olympus and left me to set out once again for the house of Circe. When I reached the gate, I cried out, and Circe invited me in. She prepared a mixture for me and when she gave it to me, I drank it off at once. She changed her tone, struck me with a rod and said, "Off to the sty with you. Go lie with your other comrades!"

As she spoke, I drew my sharp sword, rushed at her as if to kill her. She cried out loudly, fell down on her knees and begged for mercy.

"Who are you? Where do you come from? What is the name of your homeland? How could you resist the power of these drugs? No other man has been able to resist their power. But you have withstood them. Are you Odysseus, the man the gods always prophesied would come to me? Have pity on me."

I answered at once. "Circe, how can you command me to be gentle with you. You have turned my men into swine. I can have no mercy until you swear an oath that you will plot no further evil against me."

She pledged her word as I commanded. She prepared an elaborate banquet, but I couldn't eat. I sat there, brooding about many things. When Circe saw me refuse food, she said, "Odysseus, why are you sitting so quietly like a man with many problems on his mind? Do you think this is another trick? You need fear no longer. I have given my word."

"Circe," I replied, "what man could bear to feast while his companions are in bondage. If you wish me to eat, free my companions so that I can see them with my own eyes."

Circe rose and left the palace with the rod in her hand. She opened the gates of the sty and drove out my comrades—in the guise of swine. She rubbed a new drug on each. The bristles dropped away, and they became men again—younger and more handsome than ever. They recognized me at once and grasped my hand, sobbing aloud for joy. Even Circe was touched.

"Odysseus," she said at last, "go back to your ship. Draw it up to the shore; put your arms in caves, and bring all your comrades back."

I agreed. When I reached the ship, I found my men lamenting our fate. When they saw me, they fairly jumped for joy. I directed them as Circe suggested.

"Come; put all your arms into the cave nearby. Follow me at once. You'll find your comrades in the palace of Circe, having a wonderful time."

They rushed to obey me, but Eurylochus held back.

"Poor fools," he said, "where are you going? Are you looking for trouble at Circe's palace? Do you want to be turned into swine, wolves, or lions, to act as her unwilling bodyguards? Remember the last men who followed Odysseus into the cave of the Cyclops. They didn't return either."

She rubbed a new drug on each.

For a moment I thought I'd slay him on the spot, even though he was related to me. But my comrades soothed me, saying, "Come, Odysseus, we'll leave him here, if you wish. He can guard the ship. Lead us on, though, to Circe's. We're all for your plan."

They left the ship. Even Eurylochus came sheepishly after, for he feared my wrath. We found our comrades banqueting at the palace. When both groups met, they were overcome with emotion. Circe, who was standing near me, broke in:

"No more mourning, Odysseus. I know about your troubles, your adventures on the sea and land. Come; eat and drink until you become as gay as when you left Ithaca. You are not too cheerful, certainly, for you have suffered a great deal."

Thus she persuaded us. For a full year we enjoyed ourselves on the island of Circe. At the end of that time, my companions spoke to me.

"Master, if you ever expect to reach your home island again, you'd better be giving your return some thought."

I agreed. That night I again begged assistance from Circe, saying, "Fulfill your promise, O Circe, that you would send me home. My thoughts turn homeward. I long to go back."

"Very well, Odysseus," she replied, "don't stay here against your will. But there is another voyage you must take. You must go to the land of the dead. There in the kingdom of Hades and Persephone, you must consult the soul of Tiresias, a blind prophet. Even as a spirit he has wisdom and understanding."

My heart was heavy at her words. I sat down and wept. I felt there was no point in living. Turning to her I said, "Alas, Circe, who can guide me on this voyage? No one has ever gone to the land of the dead in a ship."

"I can direct you," she replied. "When you get there, dig a trench. Pour offerings to all the dead. Promise that you will make sacrifices to the spirits when you return to Ithaca. Pledge an extra sacrifice to Tiresias himself. Then sacrifice on the spot two sheep, which I will give you. Many souls will come to drink the blood of the sheep. Keep them all away until the spirit of Tiresias comes. When he comes, he will prophesy to you about your homeward voyage. He will tell how you may return over the sea."

She left me. I went through the house, arousing my comrades. "Wake up. We must be off. Circe has given us good advice."

They all obeyed. But even there we had trouble before we left. In our company was a young man named Elpenor—not too brave or intelligent. Heavy with wine he had been sleeping on the roof to keep cool. Hearing the noise of our preparation he rushed up suddenly, forgetting for the moment where he was. He fell backward off the roof, breaking his neck at once. His soul went straight to the land of the dead.

When the men had assembled, I addressed them.

"You're probably thinking that we're off for our dear native land. Circe, though, has shown us another way —we must go first to the land of the dead to consult the soul of Tiresias, the blind prophet."

Poor fellows, they began to weep.

CHAPTER SEVEN

The Land of the Dead

We set off, aided by a helpful breeze provided by Circe. We sailed on and on to the very boundaries of the ocean. Here live the Cimmerians, who dwell so far on the edge of the world that the sun never shines for them. They are always covered with night and shadow. We drew up our ship, took out the sheep, and went on along the ocean stream until we came to the place to which Circe had directed us.

I drew out my sword and dug a trench. We poured offerings to the dead. I made the promises Circe had told me to make. Then I slaughtered the sheep and let their blood flow into the trench. Immediately the souls of the dead began to flock around us, seeking once again to drink the life-giving blood. But I kept them off, waiting for the spirit of Tiresias.

As I was waiting, along came the soul of my companion Elpenor, for he was not yet buried. We had had to leave his body unburied on the island of Circe, for other jobs had urged us on. When I saw him, I wept and said, "How did you come so quickly to the gloomy West? You have come sooner on foot than I came with our swift ships!"

Mournfully he replied, "Odysseus, a bad fate and too much wine settled me. Lying down on the roof of

64

"Why did you leave the light of the sun to come into this land of gloom and death?"

Circe's palace, I forgot where I was. I fell backward off the roof and broke my neck. My soul descended at once to Hades. I have a request to make. I beg of you, in the name of your wife and family, please don't forget me when you leave. Don't leave me behind unburied and unmourned. Burn me with all my armor. Build by the seashore a monument of me for those who come after. Do all this and put my own oar above the tomb."

When he had finished, I replied, "Poor Elpenor, I promise to do all this for you."

After the spirit of Elpenor, the soul of my own mother came by. I wept to see her. But, remembering my instructions, I kept her away from the blood until the soul of Tiresias came. When the old blind prophet came at last, he recognized me at once.

"Unhappy man," he said, "what brings you here? Why did you leave the light of the sun to come into this land of gloom and death? Well, let me drink the dark blood so that I may prophesy true."

When he had drunk the blood, he turned to me and said, "You wish a pleasant voyage home, mighty Odysseus, but the gods will make that journey hard for you. I fear that you will not escape the notice of Poseidon. Remember, he is very angry with you for your treatment of his son, Polyphemus. You still have a chance of getting home safe and sound provided you can keep your companions in check. When you get to the island of Trinacria, you will find the cattle of the

Sun at pasture. *Don't touch them!* If you let them alone, you may get back to Ithaca after some minor misfortunes. If you do harm these cattle, then you'll lose ship and comrades—all of them! Even if you escape death yourself, you'll get home after many years. You'll arrive home on a foreign ship without a single comrade. You'll find troubles in your own house, men who are proud and insolent, men who seek to marry your own wife.

"True, you'll avenge yourself on the suitors, after much strife. Then if you make fitting sacrifice to Poseidon, you will still live to a ripe old age, far from the sea, happy in those around you. Far better, though, if you do not touch the cattle of the sun god."

"Ah well, Tiresias," I replied, "if the gods will have it so, I have nothing to say. But tell me this. I see over there the soul of my own mother. She merely sits by the blood and doesn't recognize me, her son. How can I have her know me?"

"If you let anyone of the dead come near the blood," he replied, "he will speak the truth. If you refuse, he will go away."

After he said this, Tiresias returned to the house of the dead. At last the shade of my mother came near and drank the dark blood. She knew me at once.

"Ah, poor son, how did you come to this land of shadows, flesh and blood that you are? Are you still wandering from Troy? Haven't you yet reached Ithaca? Haven't you seen your wife Penelope?"

"No, my mother," I replied, "I had to come here to

consult the soul of Tiresias. I have not yet reached my native land. I've had nothing but trouble since I followed Agamemnon to Troy. But come, tell me. How did you die? Was it a long disease? And tell me about my father and my son, whom I left behind. Is my property still intact? Has someone else taken over our house, thinking I am gone forever? Tell me about my good wife? Is she watching over everything? Has she married again?"

"Your wife," replied my mother, "has stayed faithful in your palace. She spends her days and nights in miserable anxiety. As yet no one has taken over your property. Your son Telemachus is a good manager. Your father stays off in the country. Old age is weakening him day by day. As for me—no, disease had nothing to do with it. My worries over you, dear Odysseus, finally killed me."

I wished to embrace my mother. Three times I threw my arms around her shade. Three times it flew from my arms like a dream. In grief I spoke to her.

"Dear mother, why don't you let me embrace you? Have the gods sent forth just an image that I may grieve?"

"Alas, my son," replied my mother, "there is no deception. All mortals are like this after death. No longer have we flesh and bones, but the soul, like a dream, goes fluttering off. Now hurry back to the light. Don't forget all this, but tell it to your wife by and by."

Then came the shades of many women, to whom I

spoke in turn. I cannot name all of them. How many wives and daughters of heroes I beheld! But it is time for sleep. For telling the rest of my story will take all night.

*　*　*

Odysseus paused in the telling of his story. All the Phaeacians were hushed in silence, spellbound by his story. Arete broke the silence.

"What do you think of our guest now, Phaeacians? Is he not a remarkable man? True, he is my guest, but you all have a share in honoring him."

One of the Phaeacians declared, "Our Queen has spoken wisely and well. What do you say, Alcinous?"

"Let the stranger stay a little longer," declared Alcinous. One more day won't matter. If he stays until tomorrow, we'll have time to bring all our gifts together."

"Most illustrious Alcinous," replied Odysseus, "if you kept me a whole year longer to heap me with gifts, I'd approve. For they will all think better of me at Ithaca if I don't come home empty handed."

"It's easy to see," said Alcinous, "that you are no thief or impostor. There are many liars thriving throughout the world. There is the ring of truth in your story. But come, we're curious to know more. Did you see, in the land of the dead, any of your comrades who were slain at Troy? The night is young. It's not time for bed yet. I could stay up all night to hear your tale."

"Mighty Alcinous, there is a time for words and a time for sleep. However, if you still wish to listen, I'm ready to tell you a story even more touching. I'll tell you about the Greeks who survived the war but were slain at home through the plotting of an evil woman."

And so Odysseus continued his story.

* * *

After the spirits of the women had departed, the soul of Agamemnon came sorrowfully to the trench. Others, who had died with him, stood around him. As soon as he drank the dark blood, he knew me. He wept loudly—and stretched forth his arms to hold me. But he had no strength in his arms. I pitied him and spoke to him.

"Glorious son of Atreus, Agamemnon, King of Men! What fate brought you to this pass? Did you go down before the blasts of Poseidon on the stormy sea? Did an enemy strike you low in some raid or battle?"

"Wise Odysseus," he replied, "Poseidon did not overcome me on the seas, nor did an enemy subdue me on land. My wife Clytemnestra, in league with Aegisthus, plotted against me and slew me at a feast. I died most cruelly. My comrades were slain around me, as swine are slaughtered for a banquet. You are used to bloodshed in battle, but the sight of this treachery would have moved you to tears. The ground reeked with blood. As I lay dying, I raised my hands in a last attempt to reach her sword. But she went off insolently, not even bothering to close my eyes though I died at her feet.

"There is nothing more terrible than a shameless woman who schemes and plots. What a horrible deed she planned, the foul murder of her own husband! I thought I was returning, a welcome sight to my children and my servants. But she has disgraced all womankind by her deeds."

I cried out, "Heaven help us. The gods have certainly been enemies of your family from the beginning, and always through the schemes of women. How many of us perished for the sake of Helen? Now you tell me that your wife Clytemnestra plotted your death from afar."

Agamemnon replied, "Let this be a lesson to you. Don't be gentle with your wife. Don't tell her all your business. Tell some things, and conceal the rest. You're lucky, though, Odysseus. Your wife is not now plotting your murder. Penelope is a gem of wisdom and good sense. When we left her to go to war, she was but a young bride with an infant at her side. He is probably a warrior himself by now. You'll be happy to see him when you return. My own wife didn't even give me a chance to see my son before she slew me. Lay your course toward your native land secretly. Women are no longer to be trusted. But come now, tell me something. Have you had any news about my son? I know he is not dead, for he has not yet come to the land of the dead."

"Alas, son of Atreus," I replied, "I don't know whether he is alive or dead."

As we stood lamenting, the soul of Achilles came by, and some of the other Greek heroes, too. Achilles knew me and said, "Here is Odysseus. What are you planning now? How did you dare to come to the land of the dead, where dwell only spirits and shades?"

"Achilles, son of Peleus," I replied, "most excellent of all the Greeks. I came for the advice of Tiresias to help me find my way back again to rocky Ithaca. I have not yet come anywhere near Greece. Wherever I go I find troubles. But you, Achilles, are the most blessed of all men who have ever lived or will live. When you lived, we honored you with the gods. Now that you are dead, you are still a power in the land of shades. Don't be sorrowful, Achilles."

"Illustrious Odysseus," he replied, "don't speak to me of death. I would rather be the lowliest person on earth *alive* than rule over all the dead. But come, tell me about my son. Did he go to the wars and become a leader? And tell me of my father Peleus. Is he still honored in his native land, or have the Greeks lost respect for him because he is weakened by age? I am no longer among the living to help him, strong as I was when I slew the greatest of the Trojans on the battle-fields of Troy. If I could go back in my former strength to my father's house, then I would make all terrified if they misused my father."

So he spoke, and I answered, "I have no news of

your noble father Peleus, but I do have news about your dear son Neoptolemus. In fact, I brought him myself from Scyros to join the Greek army. I can say truthfully that he was among the first to speak up in our counsels before the taking of Troy. His advice was excellent. Only Nestor and I were able to surpass him in debating.

"When we fought on the plains in front of Troy, he never stayed with the crowd, but always rushed on first, giving way to nobody in his fight. Many heroes he slew. How many I cannot begin to tell you. But he accounted for such powerful opponents as Eurypylus, one of the handsomest men I ever saw. And when we all got into the famous Trojan Horse and waited to rush out upon the unsuspecting Trojans, the other Greek leaders trembled with fear. *He* never even turned pale. Instead he begged me to let him leave the Trojan Horse at once, so eager was he to begin the battle. After the fall of Troy he left, laden with spoils, with not a scratch on him. Such are the fortunes of war."

After I finished speaking, the soul of mighty Achilles went off, happy that his son was so famous and brave. But other souls crowded about and told their troubles. Only one stood apart, Ajax, son of Telamon. He was still resentful toward me because I had once won a victory over him in the contest for the arms of Achilles. How I wish I had not won that contest—a contest which finally brought Ajax to the grave. *There* was a man, handsome, strong, first among the Greeks except for Achilles himself! I spoke to him.

"Ajax, son of noble Telamon, won't you forget even in death your anger toward me? Won't you forget those cursed arms? They brought nothing but evil to the Greeks, since we lost you as a result. When you died, we Greeks mourned you and honored you as much as we did great Achilles. Zeus is to blame—no one else! He hated the army of the Greeks, and he brought you low. But come here, Ajax, and hear what I have to say. Conquer your pride."

Ajax did not answer me, but went off, back among the souls of all the other dead. I'd have followed him there and insisted he speak to me, but I wished to see other souls.

Next I saw Minos, son of Zeus himself, who acts as judge and lawgiver to the dead. Then came huge Orion, playing at hunting even as he did when living. I saw Tityus, the giant. He was stretched upon the ground, helpless. Two vultures continually tore away at his liver, and he was powerless to stop them. This was his punishment for trying to kidnap Latona, wife of Zeus. And I saw Tantalus among the damned, too. He stood in a lake up to his chin. But he stood thirsting and could not drink. As often as he stooped to drink, so often the water disappeared, leaving him on dry land. From above, tall trees dangled fruit near his head—pears, apples, figs, olives, and pomegranates. Whenever the old man reached up to pluck the fruits, the wind blew them away from his grasp.

I saw Sisyphus, too. His torture was to roll up an enormous stone to the top of a hill. Just as he got it near the summit, ready to roll over, the stone rolled insolently down again to the plain. He kept trying though, despite the sweat and dirt. I saw Hercules next—just an image that is, for Hercules himself is among the immortals. Around the phantom the ghosts twittered like birds. The shade knew me at once and said, "Odysseus, son of Laertes, you're following an evil fate, just as I suffered when alive. Though my father was Zeus, I had many misfortunes and labors to perform. I was bound to a contemptible person, who gave me difficult jobs to do. Once he sent me here to Hades for the guardian watchdog, for he could not think of any labor more difficult. I did it, though. I brought the dog back to him."

Having spoken, the phantom went again to the house of shades. I stayed longer, hoping to see more of the great heroes who died before my time. But before I could see them, a great army of the dead assembled around me with frightening outcries. I was terrified. I rushed back to my ship and ordered my companions to set sail at once. The wave of the ocean stream bore us steadily along.

CHAPTER EIGHT

The Six-Headed Monster

Our ship left the ocean stream and went out into the open sea. Soon we reached Aeaea, land of the dawn and the sunrise. We drew up our ship upon the sands and disembarked. We slept on the shore until morning. Soon after sunrise I sent my comrades forward to the house of Circe to bring back the corpse of our comrade Elpenor. We buried him sorrowfully, according to the instructions his soul had given us. Having built his tomb we placed the oar over it.

Circe arrived soon after. Her attendants brought bread, meat, and wine. She stood among us and said, "What men you are! So you went down to Hades while still alive? You have the privilege of dying twice. Most other men have but one chance! Come now; eat, drink, and be merry. Tomorrow you will set sail. I'll give you full instructions to protect you from harm."

We agreed readily. We feasted and drank till sunset. When night came on, the men slept near the ship. But Circe took me by the hand away from the others and bade me sit down by her. She asked many questions about the trip, and I told it all as best I could. At last she said to me, "Good, that's over and done with.

But now listen to what I have to say and *don't forget it!*

"On your way from here you'll sail by the Sirens first of all. They are charmers. Whoever sails near and hears the song of the Sirens immediately forgets wife and children. For the Sirens, sitting in a meadow, soothe him with a piercing song. Around them is a large heap of bones of men rotting away. Sail beyond them. Fill the ears of your companions with wax for fear they should hear the Sirens' song. But you can listen if you like. Have your men tie you, hands and feet, against the mast. Then you can listen to their song safely and enjoy it. If you beg your companions to free you, instruct them in advance to tie you still tighter.

After you pass the Sirens, you have a choice of two courses. In one path you will find a pair of lofty rocks, surrounded by the waves of the sea. The gods call the rocks "the Wanderers." Not a bird can pass between them, not even the doves who are messengers of Zeus. The clashing rocks always crush them. Ships never get through these rocks. In all the years only one vessel has ever got through. That was the Argo, famous vessel of the Argonauts under Jason. Probably the Argo would have been destroyed, too, but Hera loved Jason and protected him.

"In the other direction lie two cliffs. One of them nearly touches the sky with its sharp peak. The summit is always in clouds. No man could ever climb this mountain, even if he had twenty hands and feet. The rock is smooth and polished. In the middle of this rock there is a shadowy cave toward the westward. Make for that cave, noble Odysseus. The cave is so high a strong archer could not reach it with his arrow. This is where Scylla lives, shrieking terribly. Her voice is like a new-born puppy's, it's true, but she herself is a huge monster. No one would like to meet her, I tell you, not even a god.

"She has twelve dangling feet and six long necks. On each neck there is a gruesome head, each head with three rows of teeth. She wallows in the middle of her hollow cave and pokes her heads out of the cavern. She fishes there, watching about the rock for dolphins and even whales, if they come by. No one has ever passed her unharmed. She always snatches a man from the ships with each of her heads.

"The other cliff is lower. Here there is a large wild fig-tree flourishing with leaves. Under this, Charybdis sucks in the black water. Three times a day she sucks it in, and three times a day she spouts it out. Don't be there when she sucks the water in, for then no one could save you, not even Poseidon himself. You'd better sail by Scylla. It's better to lose six of your companions than the whole ship."

"Tell me, O goddess," I said, "can I avoid Charybdis and attack Scylla when she rushes to seize my men?"

"Stubborn fool," she replied, "you're asking for

trouble. Won't you yield even to the immortal gods? Scylla cannot be killed. She is a deathless evil, terrible and difficult and fierce. You cannot fight with her. There is no defense. Flight is the only course. If you delay for a fight, she'll come back for another round of six men. Make haste through that point and pray that Scylla takes no more men.

"Next you will come to the island of Trinacria. Here are kept the oxen and sheep of the Sun God, fifty of each. They never die, and they never have young. Thy have goddesses for shepherdesses. If you leave them unharmed, you may still get to your Ithaca with some minor misfortunes. But if you harm them, then I foretell the destruction of your ship and your companions. Even if you yourself should escape, you will return late, in misfortune, without your comrades."

As she finished, the first hints of morning announced the day. She left and I went to my companions and urged them to hurry. They went aboard and sat down on the benches. They rowed mightily, assisted by a wind that fair-haired Circe had sent on behind us. After the ship was well on its way, I addressed my companions.

"My comrades, it's not right that only one or two should know what's going to happen to us. I'll tell you about our fates, so that we may be forewarned and thus avoid destruction. First, Circe warned us against the song of the Sirens. She ordered me alone to hear

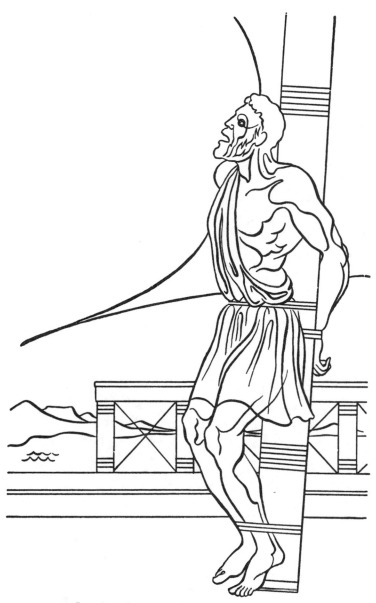

I ordered my companions to let me free.

their singing. Bind me to the mast. If I beg you and order you to loosen me, then tie me still tighter."

So I explained the prophecy to my men. Meanwhile the ship drew near to the isle of the Sirens, pushed along by a favorable breeze. Suddenly the wind stopped. The ship was becalmed. My companions rose and rolled up the sail, storing it away. They began to row, whitening the water with long strokes. Then I took out the wax and warmed it in the sun. I put some into the ears of all my companions. They bound me to the mast, tying me securely. When we were within shouting distance of the Sirens, they began a beautiful song.

"Come here, admirable Odysseus, glory of all the Greeks! Stop your ship and listen to our singing. No one has ever passed by here without stopping to listen and enjoy our songs. We know all things—what the Greeks and Trojans suffered before Troy, and we know all that will happen on this earth."

That was the message they gave. I wanted desperately to hear them. I ordered my companions to let me free, but they rowed all the faster. Two of them rose and bound me more tightly. After we had passed from earshot, my beloved comrades took away the wax and freed me.

After leaving the island behind, we saw smoke. A vast wave rolled toward us with a deafening roar. In their terror the men dropped their oars, which fell into the sea with a loud splash. The ship stopped when the oarsmen ceased rowing. I hurried through the vessel and urged on my comrades.

"Friends, we have seen misfortune face to face before. This evil is no greater than the one we experienced when the Cyclops imprisoned us in his cave. We escaped that time by my valor, wisdom, and good sense. You'll live to remember this occasion, too. Come; follow my instructions. Keep rowing strongly if you want to avoid death. And you, my pilot, keep the ship away from the smoke and the wave. Hug the cliff, or we'll surely be drowned."

They hastened to obey. But I did not mention Scylla and the danger we could not avoid. For I feared my comrades would stop rowing from terror. In the excitement I forgot Circe's warning. I began to arm myself. Fully armed at last, I went to the prow of the ship. I thought Scylla, death-dealing monster that she is, would appear at that point. I looked carefully, but saw no sign of her.

We sailed through the strait, groaning in terror. On one side somewhere was Scylla. On the other was the dread whirlpool Charybdis, sucking in the waters of the sea. As she spouted the torrent out, it bubbled up as in a kettle. Foam covered the rocky shore. When she sucked the water in, it swirled furiously. The rocks echoed with the booming noise. We gazed at Charybdis horrified, fearing our destruction at any moment.

While we were so concerned, Scylla reached forth

Scylla reached forth to snatch six of my best men.

and snatched six of my best men. I looked toward the ship and my comrades at the same time. I saw them dangling pitifully above me. They called out and addressed me by name for the last time. That was a sight I'll never forget. They had been hooked like fish.

After we had escaped the perils—both Scylla and Charybdis—we came at last to the island of the Sun God. Beautiful sheep and oxen roamed the island. When I saw them, I recalled the warnings of Tiresias and Circe, who had told me to avoid this island at any cost. I addressed my companions.

"My comrades, you have been having a hard time of it. Yet there is something else I must tell you. Both Tiresias and Circe urged me to avoid this island, no matter what other course we took. They insisted that a horrible fate lay in store for us here."

The men were despondent at my words, but Eurylochus spoke up for the others.

"Odysseus, you're a powerful man. You are never weary. Surely you must be made of iron, for you don't wish your poor comrades to go ashore to sleep. We are weary. If we disembark, we can prepare a good supper here. But you want us to go off wandering in the night again. Night is a bad time for ships. Winds come up suddenly. How can anyone escape when real hurricanes arise? Let us take a hint from the gathering dusk, and get supper ready near the ships. In the morning we can start again."

My other companions applauded his words. Then I

knew we were in for it. I turned to the men and said, "You are a majority and I must yield. However, swear on oath to me that you will not, under any circumstances, kill any of the cattle or sheep we may find there. Eat only the food that Circe gave us."

They swore an oath as I commanded, and we went ashore. After supper they grieved, thinking of the comrades they had lost to Scylla. At last they fell asleep. Toward morning Zeus raised a terrible storm. Clouds covered the earth, and night returned in earnest. We drew our ship back into a safer harbor. I called my men together and again warned them.

"My comrades, there is plenty of food and drink on shipboard. *Don't touch the oxen,* or we'll all suffer for it. These cattle belong to the God of the Sun. Nothing is hidden from him."

Once again they agreed to my words. But the unfavorable wind did not let up for a solid month. As long as they had plenty of food and drink, the men did not touch the oxen. At last, though, our provisions ran out. The men went fishing and hunting, hoping to find something to eat. Gradually hunger wore them down. I went off to pray to the gods for help to return from this island. I avoided my companions and at last fell asleep.

Once again it was Eurylochus who gave bad advice to the men.

"Listen a moment, friends; you have had a hard time. No one wants to die, but death from starvation is most horrible. Let us drive off the best of the cattle and sacrifice them to the gods. If we ever reach our native Ithaca, we will build a lofty temple to the sun god. If despite our good intentions the Sun God is still angry and destroys our ship, I prefer drowning to wasting away here on a desert island."

The other men seconded his suggestion. They rounded up the heaviest oxen and made a prayer to the gods. Then they slaughtered the beasts and made fitting sacrifices. When they were preparing the animals for eating, I awoke. I rushed to the ships and smelled the odor of burning fat. Grief-stricken, I cried out to the gods.

"O Zeus and all other gods immortal, you plotted my ruin when you made me fall asleep. My companions have committed a horrible crime."

A messenger took the news at once to the Sun God. When he heard of the slaughter of his oxen, he addressed Zeus in rage.

"O father Zeus and all other blessed gods, punish the companions of Odysseus. They have insolently slain my oxen that I loved so much. If I do not get revenge, I'll be off to Hades, and shine among the dead —not among the living."

"O God of the Sun," replied Zeus the cloudgatherer, "continue to shine for the benefit of gods and men. I shall take care of Odysseus, striking his ship with a thunderbolt in the middle of the sea."

I heard all this later from Calypso, who declared she had had it from Hermes.

When I came to the ship, I scolded the men, but

there was nothing for me to do. The cattle were all dead. Then amazing things began to happen. The meat began to make noises, as of the lowing of cattle. The skins crawled. But my companions ate. For six days they continued to feast. On the seventh day the tempest stopped, and we sailed off once more.

After we had left the island, we saw no more land. Zeus brought a black cloud over our ship. The very sea became dark underneath it. The winds began to rise. The storm broke. The mast was split. As it fell, it crushed the pilot's head. The tackle fell into the hold in utter confusion. Zeus thundered and sent a bolt which struck the ship. It was whirled round and round. All my companions were thrown off the ship. They bobbed up and down on the waves like seagulls. I tried to keep going until the storm tore the sides from the keel, which a rolling wave bore along useless. I lashed together keel and mast and rode upon them, drifting before the terrible winds.

The west wind stopped abruptly, and the south wind sprang up. This was no comfort to me, for I realized it would bring me directly back to Scylla and Charybdis. All night long I drifted. At sunrise I came again to Charybdis. She gulped down the briny sea water, but I held on to a tall fig-tree, which hung over the whirlpool. I couldn't climb up into the tree, and I couldn't climb down; there was no place for me to go. So I had to hold on until Charybdis spouted up the mast and keel again. How I longed for the reappearance of my makeshift raft as I hung on, but it took a long time! At last it came. I put down my feet and hands and fell back onto the planks. I began to paddle with my hands.

Fortunately Scylla did not appear, or I'd certainly have been lost. I drifted along for nine days. On the tenth I drifted to the island of Ogygia, where the goddess Calypso lives. She nursed me back to health. There I stayed for eight long years. The rest you know. Why should I tell you what you know already?

* * *

And so Odysseus concluded his tale before the Phaeacians.

CHAPTER NINE

Back to Ithaca

After Odysseus finished, all were silent, spellbound. Alcinous broke the silence by turning to Odysseus and saying, "Well, Odysseus, since you have come to my house, I think that you will get home safely at last, despite your wanderings. And to you, Phaeacian princes, I propose that we add a large tripod and kettle to the gifts we have already given to the stranger."

The others agreed and went back to their homes. In the morning they assembled by the ship with welcome bronze gifts. They went to Alcinous's and prepared a feast. All day they banqueted. Demodocus entertained the feasters. But Odysseus kept looking at the shining sun, eager for it to set. He was anxious to be on his way.

At sunset Odysseus turned to Alcinous and said, "O most glorious king, please drink your toasts now and send me on unharmed. Everything is ready. The escort has been prepared, and the gifts have been made. May I find everything safe when I return. May those of you who stay here make your own wives and children happy. May the gods help you to prosper and keep the people from harm."

The Phaeacians approved the speech and urged the

king to send the stranger on as he wished. Alcinous ordered the herald to prepare the toast. Then Odysseus rose up and placed a cup in the hands of Queen Arete.

"Farewell, O queen," he said, "may good luck follow you all your life, until old age and death come, as they do to all of us. I am going. Bless you, your house, your children, your people, and their King Alcinous!"

As he spoke Odysseus went over the threshold. Alcinous sent with him a messenger to escort him to the ship. Arete sent women servants along, with clothing and food and drink. When they came to the ship, they put aboard all the gifts and provisions. They prepared a blanket and sheet on the deck for Odysseus, so that he might sleep soundly.

Odysseus got aboard and lay down in silence. The Phaeacian oarsmen got into their places. They loosened the cable and off they rowed. Odysseus fell asleep almost at once. His sleep was dreamless and restful. The ship seemed to fly forward, so swiftly did it go. The prow lifted out of the water, and the furrow rushed off behind. The ship went on steadily and safely. The swiftest bird would have been outdistanced. So on it sped, bearing a man with wisdom equal to the gods'. Though he had suffered many troubles, in war and on the sea, he slept fearlessly, forgetful of the past. As the morning star arose, the ship neared the island of Ithaca.

The pilot chose a sheltered harbor and guided the

ship close to shore. The men went ashore and carried Odysseus, still asleep, and placed him on the sand. They took all the gifts he had received and placed them near Odysseus—but off the beaten path in case some wanderer should come upon them while Odysseus slept. Homeward they turned, but Poseidon did not forget the threats he had made against Odysseus. He asked Zeus what he intended to do.

"Father Zeus," he declared, "I shall never be respected among the immortals, for men no longer honor me. Even the Phaeacians, who are of my own family, do not honor me. I pledged that Odysseus should have a hard time of it before getting back home. I couldn't keep him from returning altogether, since you had pledged his eventual return. But the Phaeacians not only got him home safely. They gave him more gifts of bronze and gold than he would ever have taken from Troy if he had returned unharmed with his share of the booty."

But Zeus, the cloud-gatherer, replied, "Oh no, Poseidon, what are you saying? The gods do not dishonor you! It would be a shame to insult the oldest and most respected among us. If any man does not honor you, well then you have the power of revenge. Do whatever you wish in this matter."

"I would have punished those Phaeacians on the spot," declared Poseidon, "but I always fear your sudden temper. This is what I plan to do: to destroy the beautiful Phaeacian ship on its way home from Ithaca. I want to teach them a lesson and stop them at once from ever convoying travelers safely back home. Then I plan to raise a ring of mountains around their city."

"A good idea," agreed Zeus. "Why not wait until the people are watching the ship sail into the harbor? Then turn the ship into stone near the shore that all men may marvel at it. Afterwards place your ring of mountains around the island."

Poseidon hurried off to the land of the Phaeacians and waited. As the swift Phaeacian ship sped near its homeland, Poseidon the Earth-Shaker turned it into stone and rooted it firmly to the bottom with one blow. Then he went off.

The Phaeacians were astounded and spoke to each other, "Good heavens, who has bound our swift ship while it was driving along at full speed? It was there just a moment ago!"

Alcinous sadly turned to his people and said, "Alas, I see now that the old prophecies are coming true after all. My father used to tell me that one day Poseidon would be angry with us because we keep so many ships safely out of his grasp. He said that some time Poseidon would destroy a beautiful Phaeacian ship on its return from convoy duty. He foretold that a great mountain would ring our city. I am afraid he was right. Come; do what I say and we may yet stop part of the doom. Let us provide no more convoys for strangers. We shall sacrifice twelve bulls to Poseidon, hoping that he may pity us and not put the ring of mountains around our city."

They got busy at once, prepared the sacrifices, and prayed aloud to King Poseidon.

Back in Ithaca Odysseus awoke on the shores of his native land. But he did not realize where he was. The goddess Athena covered the place with a mist, for she wanted to tell Odysseus the true state of affairs and disguise him. She did not wish his wife and friends to recognize him until he had punished the suitors who were annoying his wife by their evil acts. So it was that everything looked strange to Odysseus.

He stood up at once and looked at his native land, but there was no recognition. He cried aloud and lamented, "More trouble! What country have I come to now? Are the inhabitants cruel savages, or are they gentle and friendly? What will I do with all these gifts? Where can I go from here? I should have stayed with the Phaeacians. At least then I might have come to another powerful king, who would have brought me home safely to Ithaca.

"I just don't know what to do with all these gifts. I can't leave them here, for somebody will steal them. Really, the Phaeacian leaders were unjust to take me to another place. They promised to take me to Ithaca, and they failed to. I hope Zeus punishes them for neglecting their duties to strangers. I'll just check these possessions to see whether they took anything away with them."

He began to count all the gifts and found none missing. But he was very homesick for his own country and began to weep aloud. Then Athena came to him, dressed as a young shepherd. Odysseus was glad to see her and went up to her.

"O friend," he said, "greetings to you. You're the first one I've seen in this country. Please do me no wrong, I beg of you. Be kind enough to answer my questions truthfully. What country is this? What people live here? Is it an island in the west, or is it part of the mainland?"

"You are foolish, stranger," replied Athena, "or else you have come from a great distance. Nearly all men know about this land. It is a rugged place, no place for horses, but it is not a barren place either. It's not very big; yet it grows wheat aplenty, with abundant rainfall. It is good pasture land for goats and oxen. You'll find all kinds of wood here. As a matter of fact the name of Ithaca is known as far away as Troy—and that's a good distance from Greece."

Odysseus was glad indeed to be back on his own native soil. But he did not reply truthfully, for he thought it best to make up a story while seeing how things were.

"Yes, I heard of Ithaca, even in Crete, which is far away. Now I have come here with all these goods. I left as good a store for my sons when I left Crete,

exiled for having slain Orsilochus, son of Idomeneus.
You see, Orsilochus wanted to take away all my booty
from Troy. I couldn't stand for that. So I slew him in
ambush.

"It was a dark night, and no one knew I had slain
him. But I sought out a trading vessel and gave some
of my loot to the captain. I asked that he take me to
Pylos or Elis, but we were blown off our course. We
strayed into this port and came off the ship to sleep.
I fell into a very deep sleep. They took out all the
possessions you see and put them down beside me on
the sand. They left for Sidonia, and here I am with
all my troubles."

As he finished, the blue-eyed goddess Athena smiled
and stroked him gently. Once again she became a
woman in form, tall and majestic. She came to the
point immediately.

"A man would have to be very clever to get the
better of you in trickery, Odysseus! You would even
give a *god* a bit of trouble! Even in your own country
you cannot resist tall stories and cunning tales, which
you love so much!

"Come, let us drop all pretenses. We are both good
tricksters. You lead all mortals in trickery. I am famous among the gods for the same qualities. Did you
not recognize me, Athena, the daughter of Zeus? I
stood by you in all your troubles. I secured a welcome
for you among the Phaeacians. I am here again to

help you, to give you some good advice and to hide these gifts for you. I am going to tell you what troubles lie still ahead of you. You will have to suffer these troubles in silence, for you cannot tell anyone about them—at least not yet."

"O goddess," replied Odysseus, "it is not easy to recognize you, no matter how clever a person may be. You can take on so many disguises! But this I know well. You were always my friend while we Greeks were fighting Troy. However, after we left Troy in ruins I no longer saw you or felt you near. I thought you had forgotten me and left me to my fate. I went wandering about, overwhelmed by troubles, until the gods freed me at last. That was before you spoke to me in the land of the Phaeacians and guided me into the city. But now I beg of you, for my father's sake— I just don't believe this is Ithaca, as you say. It looks like some strange land. I think you're leading me on, deceiving me. Tell me the truth: is this really Ithaca?"

"Ah, that is just like you!" replied Athena. "That is why I cannot desert you, in all your troubles, because you are so civilized, intelligent, and ready for anything! Any other man, after so long an absence abroad, would be rushing to see his wife and children. But you wait to make sure of your own wife by your own eyes. I can tell you this about her: she is faithful to you, mourning day and night for your return.

"I always knew that you would return at last, although you would lose all your comrades. But I did not wish to struggle against my uncle Poseidon. He was angry with you because you had blinded his son Polyphemus. Come, I shall show you Ithaca to convince you. Over here is the port of Phorcys. This is the olive tree at the head of the harbor. And over here is the cave where you offered so many sacrifices to the nymphs. And there is Neritos, the wooded mountain."

As she spoke the goddess scattered the cloud. The earth appeared, and Odysseus was glad to recognize his own country. He kneeled down and kissed the fertile plain. Then he lifted up his hands and prayed to the nymphs, goddesses of streams and fountains.

"O nymphs, daughters of Zeus, I never thought that I'd see you again. Accept these prayers. I'll continue to make offerings to you, as I did years ago, if the gods allow me to live and my son to grow."

Athena broke in. "Take courage and don't worry. Come, now, let us hide the gifts in the back of the cave for safekeeping. Then we can plan what to do next."

They hid all the gifts, and Athena placed a stone against the opening. Then they sat down and plotted the downfall of the insolent suitors, who were annoying Penelope, wife of Odysseus. Athena spoke first.

"Odysseus, consider the best way of laying hands on the villains. For three years now they have been lording it in your house, wooing your wonderful wife, and giving her bridal gifts. They all think you are dead. But Penelope has never given up hope for your return. She allows them all to hope. She gives promises to all, but her heart is with you."

Odysseus replied, "If it were not for you, O goddess, I'd have been slain in my palace as Agamemnon was. It's lucky for me that you told me what to expect. Please help once more. Advise me how to get revenge upon them. Stay with me and give me courage for the fight—as you did when I fought before Troy. If you were with me, O Athena, I would fight three hundred men!"

"I will stay with you," replied Athena. "I will not forget you when we have begun the task. I have a feeling that some of those suitors will be spilling their own blood on the ground before long! For now I will disguise you so that no one will know you. I will make you an older man, wrinkle your skin and take away your auburn hair. I will give you an old cloak to wear, so worn that no one would want to wear it. I will take away the life from your beautiful eyes. When I have finished, no one will think you attractive, neither the suitors nor your wife and son.

"The first one you will meet will be the swineherd, Eumaeus. He has always been loyal toward you. He loves your son and faithful Penelope. He will be among his swine. They are near the Raven's Rock and the Spring of Arethusa. Go to him and make inquiries.

At present your son Telemachus is in Sparta, looking for news of you. I shall go to Sparta and bring Telemachus home."

"Why didn't you tell him," asked Odysseus, "since you knew all about it? Did you want him to wander over the seas, as I did, stricken with grief? Here the suitors are eating up all his wealth."

"Do not worry about him," replied Athena. "I guided him there myself so that he might win some renown in the world. He is living well. It is true that some of the suitors are waiting to ambush him before he gets back here. But I think they will be dead and buried long before they can kill him."

As she finished, Athena touched him with a rod. His skin became old and withered. He was bent over and bald. His eyes became bleared and lifeless. And she put around him an old dirty cloak. She gave him a battered old bag, full of holes. Then she left him, speeding off for Sparta to bring about the return of Odysseus son.

CHAPTER TEN

Odysseus and the Swineherd

Odysseus went up from the shore and found the hut of the swineherd. There he saw Eumaeus sitting in front of his little home. The dogs, which Eumaeus used as watchdogs, set up a barking when they saw Odysseus, and ran toward him. Odysseus dropped his stick and sat down at once. Even then he might have been assaulted if Eumaeus had not appeared on the scene. The swineherd scolded the dogs and sent them off with a shower of stones.

He turned to Odysseus and said, "Old man, you've had a narrow escape. In another moment the dogs would have finished you. You'd have cursed me then —poor me. For I have enough sorrow as it is. Every day I mourn for my noble master Odysseus, and I have to stay here raising pigs for others to eat. Poor fellow, he's probably wandering on foreign soil alone—that is, if he's still alive. But come, old man, into the hut. Eat first, and then tell me where you came from and what troubles you've had."

The swineherd led Odysseus into the hut. He made Odysseus sit down on a couch he prepared for him. Odysseus was glad to be received so well, and said, "May Zeus grant you every prayer because you have treated me so well."

"O stranger," replied the swineherd, "I couldn't mistreat a stranger, even if he were older and weaker than you. All strangers are under the protection of Zeus. I can't give you much, but it will be something. Servants must be watchful when they are under young new masters. The gods have surely hindered the return of my master, who loved me dearly and would have treated me decently. Ah, I fear he has died. I wish the whole race of Helen had perished, since she was the cause of so much bloodshed. My master went off to the Trojan War, you know, under the leadership of Agamemnon."

After he finished, the swineherd went into the yard and selected two young pigs for dinner. He slaughtered them and prepared them for the fire. After he had roasted them, he gave Odysseus a good portion and declared, "Eat, stranger, the young pigs I can offer. The well-fattened swine are kept for the suitors, who have no fear of god or pity. Even marauders and pirates have the fear of god in them. But not these men! They are certain the master is dead and are consuming all his wealth, not just one or two beasts a day!"

As he spoke, Odysseus ate hungrily. But he said nothing as he plotted destruction for the suitors. When he had eaten, the swineherd filled his own cup and gave it to Odysseus filled with wine. Odysseus took it happily, saying, "Friend, who is this powerful and

"Odysseus will return."

wealthy owner that you speak about? You say that he died for the honor of Agamemnon. Tell me his name again. Perhaps I know him. Perhaps I can give you some news of him."

"Oh no, old man," replied the swineherd, "no traveler with news of that man could make his wife and son believe it. Every wandering beggar in search of a free meal tells lies about my master. My mistress weeps at their tales, after feeding and entertaining them. You'd probably invent one yourself, old man. By now he is probably dead, and the birds have torn the skin from his bones. Or else he has become food for the fish in the sea. So he died over there and we all grieve for him—most of all do I mourn for him. I'll never find another master like him, no matter where I go, not even if I came again to my father's house. I long for my parents less than I mourn for Odysseus. I don't like to mention his name, old man, though he is not here. For he loved me and cared for me. I still think of him as my beloved lord."

Odysseus replied, "Since you have your mind made up that Odysseus will never return, I will not merely *say* but will *say with an oath* that Odysseus will return. When he returns, I'll claim my reward for bringing good news. Before that time I'll take nothing, though I am penniless. I hate like the gates of Hades the man who is forced by poverty to tell a lie. Zeus be my witness that all will turn out as I say: Odysseus will come back here this year. Before another month he will be here to take revenge upon those who dishonor his family and him."

But Eumaeus said, "Ah well, old man, I'll never pay a reward for that good news; Odysseus will never return again. Drink in peace. Let's talk of something else. Don't remind me. I am unhappy whenever anyone mentions the good Odysseus. Never mind the oath, but I do hope that Odysseus does come as all of us pray he will. I worry, too, about the son of Odysseus, Telemachus. I hoped he'd be as great a man as his father, but some god must have touched his wits. Off he went in search of news of his father. And now the suitors are waiting to ambush him on his homeward journey.

"Well, so much for him. Now, old man, tell me about yourself. Who are you? Where did you come from? What city protected you? Who were your parents? In what kind of ship did you come here? How did the sailors bring you to Ithaca? I don't imagine you walked here!"

Odysseus replied with a tall story.

"I'll tell you truthfully what happened. Even if we had a year's supply of food and drink, I couldn't tell you all my troubles. Son of a wealthy man, I came to Crete. I married a worthy wife. In war I was a great fighter. But I didn't care for work or housekeeping. I liked ships, spears, arrows—things which make others shudder. Even before the Trojan War I commanded a fleet against foreign enemies nine times. I was always successful. My power and wealth increased. I was respected by all Cretans.

"However, when Zeus determined on the Trojan War the Cretans ordered me and Idomeneus to take command of the ships to Troy. For nine years we waged war. In the tenth we destroyed Troy and set off for home. Then Zeus planned misfortune for me. I was happy only a month with my wife and parents before I decided to sail to Egypt. I equipped nine ships easily. For six days my companions feasted. On the seventh we sailed under clear skies from Crete. We reached Egypt in five days. I harbored the ships and ordered my comrades to stay with their vessels. But they foolishly destroyed the beautiful Egyptian fields and slew the men.

"The Egyptians came out to the attack in force. My men were routed. Many were killed. Some were made captive. I was taken before the king. He had pity on me and saved my life. For seven years I lived in Egypt and was given many gifts. Then along came a Phoenician who persuaded me to go with him to Phoenicia. I stayed with him a whole year. At the end of a year he set me aboard a ship going to Libya. He pretended that I was to be a partner in his business. Actually he intended to sell me as a slave. I went through necessity, though I suspected him. Soon after we had passed Crete and left it behind, a terrible storm sprang up. A thunderbolt split the ship and sank it. I was able to get hold of the mast. I clung to it for nine days, drifting through the high seas. On the tenth night a wave washed me ashore on the land of the Thesprotians. The king of the country entertained me royally. And he gave me many presents.

"It was there that I heard of Odysseus. The king declared that he had entertained him generously on his way back to his native land. And he showed me all the presents that Odysseus had collected. Odysseus had said that he was going to a sacred shrine to ask for advice about his return. The king swore that the ship was launched and the men were ready to take Odysseus back to Ithaca. He said goodbye to me when a vessel came along. He ordered the men to return me to my home, but they had other plans. They took off my rich garments and planned to sell me into slavery. They put on these rags you now see.

"By evening they had reached Ithaca. They bound me on the ship and went ashore to eat, but I was able to free myself. I wrapped my head in rags and got down from the ship by the rudder. I swam to shore away from them. Soon I was far away from them and crouched in some bushes. Meanwhile, they had discovered my escape and were shouting after me. They ran about for a while. Then they decided it was no use to hunt further. They set off again and left me here. I walked off and found your hut. I think my number isn't up yet!"

"Poor old man," declared Eumaeus, "you have

made me suffer with you in all your troubles. But I don't believe what you said about Odysseus—and you can't persuade me. Why must you tell so many lies? The gods must hold a grudge against him, or they'd have let him die nobly in battle or in the arms of his friends. Then the Greeks would have built him a fitting monument, and he'd have been famous ever after. Now he has just disappeared.

"As for me, I mind my own business here among the swine. I never go to the city unless Penelope asks me to, when some news has come. The others all sit around, asking every detail—both those who are sorry he isn't here and those who are glad. These latter eat up all his wealth boldly. I don't ask any more ever since an Aetolian told me a lie. He said that he had seen Odysseus with Idomeneus in Crete, repairing his ships which the storm had tossed around. He said that Odysseus would return, if not by summer, then surely by fall. That was a lie! Now you, poor old man, don't try to make me feel good by telling me lies. If you do, I'll have no respect for you, nor will I feed you."

Odysseus replied, "You certainly are an unbelieving fellow. You're the only one I've never been able to persuade by pledging my word. Let's make a bargain, with the gods as witness. If your master does return as I say, then send me back to my home. If he does not come, then throw me from a cliff as a warning to other favor-seekers."

"That would certainly give me a good name for

hospitality!" answered Eumaeus. "Well, it's time for supper. My companions will soon be here. Let's prepare a good meal."

Soon the other swineherds arrived. Eumaeus ordered the men to bring in the best of the pigs for sacrifice. When they had, he slaughtered it and prayed to all the gods that Odysseus might soon return. Then all the men began to eat, as portions were allotted to each.

During the evening a cold wind blew and Odysseus felt the need of another cloak. He thought he'd hint for someone to give him additional clothing. He began to speak.

"Listen a moment, Eumaeus and the rest of you. I must tell you this tale. Ah, if I were only as young and strong as I was when we planned an ambush against Troy. There were three of us appointed as leaders: Odysseus, Menelaus, and I. They needed me with them. When we came to the city, we crouched near the fortifications, among the bushes. Ah, wasn't it cold that night! Ice formed on our very shields. All the others had cloaks and other warm clothing. They slept snugly. But I had foolishly left my cloak behind, not expecting such cold. I was skimpily dressed, I can tell you!

"Night was well on toward morning, when I nudged Odysseus, who was near me, with my elbow. 'Odysseus,' I said, 'I won't be alive much longer I'm afraid this weather has me shivering with the cold. It'll soon

be all up with me.' Odysseus immediately had a plan—
he always was a great planner and fighter!

"Speaking in a low voice he said to me, 'Ssshhh;
don't let any of the other Greeks hear you.' Propped
up on one elbow he said aloud, 'Listen, friends, I've
just had a frightening dream. We're alone here, a
long way from the ships. I do wish somebody would
go off to Agamemnon to send us some reinforcements.'

"After he had finished, one of the Greeks got up,
threw off his cloak, and ran off to the ships. How
warm that cloak was for me! If I were only as young
again!"

Eumaeus spoke up. "That's a good story, old man,
and quite to the point! You'll get your cloak for to-
night. In the morning, though, you'll have to put on
your own cloak again. There aren't too many to go
around. Each man has but one. When Odysseus' son
returns, he'll give you all the clothing you need, and
he'll send you on your way as well."

When he had spoken, he jumped up and prepared
a warm bed for Odysseus near the fire. He spread a
warm cloak over him, and Odysseus slept. But Eumaeus went out to sleep near the swine, to protect
them. Odysseus was happy to see how the old man
protected his master's interests in his absence.

CHAPTER ELEVEN

The Return of Telemachus

Meanwhile Athena had gone to Sparta to induce Telemachus to return home again. In the house of Menelaus she found Telemachus with his friend, the son of Nestor. The latter was sound asleep, but Telemachus could not rest, for all through the night worry over his father kept him awake. Standing near him, Athena spoke.

"O Telemachus, there is no longer any point in your wandering away from home, leaving your possessions in the hands of insolent men. If you stay away much longer, they will have divided all your wealth. Urge your host to send you home as quickly as possible to help your mother. Everyone back home is trying to persuade her to marry the wealthiest suitor. You know how women are. They like to bring wealth to the men they marry, forgetting their former husband and children.

"This is something else you should know. Several of the suitors are lying in wait to ambush you and kill you. They are staying in the strait of Ithaca, ready to pounce upon you. On your way back take a different route. Come home at night. Beach your ship. Go directly to the hut of the swineherd. Stay there for the rest of the night. In the morning have him send a message to Penelope that you are safely home."

When she had finished, Athena went off to Olympus. In the morning Telemachus addressed his host.

"O Menelaus," he declared, "chief of all the people, please send me back to my own land. I am very anxious to return."

Menelaus replied, "I'll not keep you here, Telemachus, since you are so eager to return. It is equally bad taste to keep a guest who wants to go, or to hurry off a guest who'd like to stay. But wait just a while longer till I can present gifts to you and prepare a banquet. It is a good idea to eat well before setting forth on a journey. If you'd like to see some of the countryside before you go, I'd be glad to go along with you as a guide."

"No, Menelaus," said Telemachus, "I'd prefer to return at once. When I left, I appointed no guardian over my wealth."

Menelaus immediately ordered his wife, the famous Helen of Troy, to prepare a feast and assemble gifts for Telemachus. Menelaus himself gave his guest a gold and silver bowl of rare beauty. Helen presented him with a splendid robe.

After the elaborate banquet. Menelaus bade him farewell.

In reply Telemachus declared, "I hope that when I reach Ithaca I'll be able to tell Odysseus all about your kindness and the presents you gave to me."

As he spoke a bird flew over to the right, an eagle with a white goose in its talons. The eagle swooped near them. All the onlookers were glad. Nestor's son declared, "Menelaus, is this a good omen, do you think?"

While he pondered a moment, Helen broke in. "Let me speak, and I will make a prophecy as the gods have told me. Just as this eagle came from the mountain and snatched away the goose, so will Odysseus return at last and be revenged upon the suitors. Perhaps he's already there!"

"May Zeus bring this about!" declared Telemachus. "If it happens and I am there, I'll honor you as a goddess."

Off went Telemachus to his ship, escorted by Nestor's son. They placed in the vessel all the gifts that Telemachus had been given. Farewells were made, and Telemachus sailed off with his men.

Meanwhile Odysseus was taking his meal in the hut of the swineherd. Odysseus spoke to Eumaeus, to see whether he'd keep him on in the hut or send him to the city.

"Listen, Eumaeus and all the rest of you. At dawn I plan to go to the city to beg, so that I will no longer be a burden to you. Please direct me there. Perhaps someone will give me a little bread and wine. When I reach the house of Odysseus, I'll tell my news to Penelope. I'll mix with those insolent suitors to see whether I can get a meal out of them. They evidently have a lot to eat. I'll tell you: there's no other man who can keep a fire going as well as I can, who can carve, roast and pour out wine as I can."

Eumaeus spoke sadly, "Good heavens, stranger, what made you say that? Are you looking for an early grave? That's what you'll get if you go to the suitors, whose insolence and violence cry out to heaven. Their servants are somewhat different from you—young men, handsome and well groomed! The tables are always filled with bread, meat and wine. Why don't you stay here? You're hurting no one by your presence. My companions and I don't mind. When Telemachus comes back, he'll provide you a new set of clothes. Besides he'll send you wherever you want to go."

Odysseus replied, "I hope you're as dear to Zeus as you are to me, good Eumaeus. You've taken a load off my mind. There is nothing worse for us mortals than drifting about. These greedy stomachs of ours get us into a lot of trouble. Well, since you ask me to stay here until Telemachus comes, tell me about Odysseus' mother and father. Are they alive or dead?"

"Stranger," declared Eumaeus, "I'll tell you this, Laertes, Odysseus' father, is still alive. He constantly prays to Zeus for death. He grieves constantly for his missing son and for his wife, who died not long ago. She died through worry over her son—a death I'd like to see no one have. While she lived, I liked to visit her, to ask her the news. For I was almost one of the family. I miss her gentle words—little enough kindness I get these days."

"I am amazed to hear all this, Eumaeus," declared Odysseus. "You must have been a little fellow when you were taken away from your country and your own parents. Tell me of your experiences. Was your home city destroyed? Did pirates capture you? Were you sold thus into slavery?"

"Well, stranger," replied Eumaeus, "since you want to know my story, listen while you sip your wine. There's no point in going to bed too early. Too much sleep can be a bother, too. If you other fellows prefer, you can sleep outside. We'll stay in here and talk. There's comfort in sharing a tale of troubles—after the troubles are over and done with. Here's the story.

"There's a certain island called Syria—not a large island, but a good pasture land. The land is fertile and the people never want for anything. Disease is practically unknown. Most people die of old age. There are two cities on the island. My father ruled both.

"One day some Phoenician traders stopped off, tricky fellows, always with loads of trinkets and the like. One of the women in my father's house was a Phoenician woman. She was eager to return to her home land, and so she made a bargain with the traders. To pay for her passage she would kidnap me. I'd bring a good price in the slave markets, she said. They stayed with us a long time, making many purchases and building up their stock. One day, when they were ready to sail, the woman led me off. I followed her in my innocence. She stole all she could besides and put the loot aboard with me.

"They put to sea. We sailed six days. On the seventh the Phoenician woman died suddenly. They threw her out to the fishes, leaving me sad indeed. Soon the vessel approached Ithaca. Here Laertes bought me, and here I stayed."

"That's a sad story, indeed," declared Odysseus. "Your troubles have moved me deeply. Still you've had some good mixed with your misfortune. You did come to the house of a mild man, a gentleman who treats you well. You do live a good life. Now I—I come here after wandering and drifting."

So the two men conversed. They had little sleep, for morning came soon.

On the shore, at the same time, the companions of Telemachus were beaching their ship and casting out the anchor. After they had breakfasted on the shore, Telemachus spoke.

"Sail the ship into the harbor. I'm off to the country to see some of my shepherds. In the evening, after my tour of inspection, I'll see you at the city. Tomorrow I'll pay you your wages and give you a feast besides."

One of the men asked, "Where shall we stay? At

whose house shall we stay? Shall we go directly to your mother's?"

"I wish I could invite you to my house," declared Telemachus. "I'd like to entertain you royally. But you'd better not go until I get there. You won't be able to see my mother, anyhow, for she keeps herself secluded. Very few of the suitors ever see her. She constantly weaves by herself in one of the upper rooms. There is someone I can direct you to, though. Go to Eurymachus. He is about the best of the suitors, very eager to win my mother. But Zeus will have something to say about that!"

While he spoke a bird flew on the right of him, a hawk with a dove in its talons. Theoclymenus, a prophet, turned to Telemachus.

"Telemachus, this is a good sign. The gods didn't send this omen for nothing. Yours is the royal house. The sign must apply to you."

"I do hope so!" exclaimed Telemachus. "If it turns out so, then I'll heap gifts upon you."

Then Telemachus went on board ship and ordered the men to set sail for the city's harbor. Telemachus himself put on fine sandals, grasped his spear, and left the vessel. The men sailed off to the city, while Telemachus set off at once for the hut of Eumaeus the swineherd.

CHAPTER TWELVE

Telemachus Meets His Father

During all this, Odysseus and the swineherd were preparing their meal in the hut. They had lit their fire and sent the other herdsmen out to pasture the swine. As Telemachus approached the hut, the same dogs who had attacked Odysseus wagged their tails in a friendly way. The dogs did not bark or attack the newcomer. When Odysseus saw the strange behavior of the dogs, he said, "Eumaeus, some friends of yours must be coming. Look at the dogs. I've never seen them so gentle."

Scarcely had he finished speaking when Telemachus himself stood outside the hut. The swineherd was so astonished he dropped the bowl he was holding. He went up to Telemachus and fell down on his knees before him. He embraced him as a father would after long absence. At last Eumaeus spoke.

"Telemachus, you're back at last! I thought I'd never see you again since you went off to sea. Come in; come in. Let me feast my eyes on you. You come here little enough as it is. You spend most of your time watching those villainous suitors."

"Of course, my good friend," replied Telemachus.

"I've come here for two reasons: to see you again and to find out whether my mother is married again or not."

"No," replied Eumaeus, "she is as faithful to your father as ever. She spends all her time weeping for him."

Telemachus entered the hut. As he approached, Odysseus rose to give him his seat, but Telemachus said, "Stay where you are, stranger. I'll find another seat. Eumaeus here will provide one."

The swineherd prepared a meal for Telemachus, who had sat down opposite Odysseus. After breakfast, Telemachus turned to Eumaeus and asked, "Where did this stranger come from? Who were the sailors who brought him here? He surely didn't walk here!"

Eumaeus replied, "This is his story. He claims to be from Crete. He says that he has been wandering over the wide world. He escaped from some Thesprotians and came here. He is yours to do with as you will. He begs assistance of you."

"Ah, Eumaeus," declared Telemachus, "you make me sad to hear you. How can I receive him in my own house? I am young and don't trust myself to stand up to an angry opponent. My mother is confused whether to stay here with me or to take another husband. Since the stranger has come here, I'll give him a cloak and other beautiful garments. I'll give him sandals and a two-edged sword. I'll send him wherever he seeks to go.

THE ODYSSEY

"Meanwhile, please keep him here, if you will. I'll send clothing and food—so that you poor fellows won't lose out on your rations. I won't allow him to go among the suitors, for they're too dangerously bold. They may make fun of him and make me sad. It's difficult for one man to stand up against them, so numerous are they."

But Odysseus said, "My friend, I hope you'll pardon my saying something. I am very annoyed to hear how the suitors are treating a fine fellow like you. Are you a willing victim? Are the people against you? Are your brothers to blame?

"Ah, if I were as young as you! If I were the son of Odysseus, wouldn't I go into the hall and raise a rumpus! I'd make them sorry for their deeds! Even if, with their superior numbers, they slew me on the spot, at least I'd die honorably under my own roof. I'd rather have that than have to watch them act in their insulting way."

"Stranger," replied Telemachus, "this is the whole story. The people are not against me. I have no brothers to find fault with. I am an only child. My great-grandfather had one son. My grandfather had one son. My father had only one, too. My family goes by ones, you see. Odysseus left me a mere infant, an only son.

"That's why we have so many enemies to worry about now. All the neighboring chieftains are wooing my mother and wasting our wealth. She cannot refuse outright. She doesn't want to marry, if she can help it. So the suitors go on their merry way, gobbling up our possessions. Well, it's up to the gods.

"Eumaeus, please go to Penelope at once. Tell her I've arrived safely home. I'll stay here. Don't tell anybody but Penelope. Don't let any of those Greeks know. They are planning enough evils against me as it is."

Eumaeus replied, "I know. I see all these things. You're speaking to one who understands the whole business. Come, now, tell me something. Shall I go to tell Laertes, too, poor old man? He's wasting away, scarcely eating a thing for worry."

"That's a shame, I know," declared Telemachus. "But we'll have to leave him sorrowing for now. If all of us got what we wished, we'd choose my father's return promptly. Give your message, and have your mistress send out the old housekeeper to tell him. You come directly back."

Eumaeus set out at once. Soon after he started Athena appeared in the person of a fine tall woman, and stood at the entrance of the hut. While remaining invisible to Telemachus, she made herself visible to Odysseus—for the gods are able to do this, you know. Odysseus and the dogs saw her. The dogs didn't bark, but crawled away in terror. Odysseus left the hut and followed her. When they were a distance away, she spoke.

"*I am your father.*"

"Odysseus, it is time to tell your son. Reveal yourself; tell him of the destruction we have planned for the suitors. When the battle against them is raging, I will not be far away!"

As she spoke Athena touched him with her staff. She clothed him in clean robes. She made him more like the Odysseus of old. Once again he was dark, tanned, young, and strong. She left him, and he went into the hut. Telemachus was startled. In terror he looked away, fearing that this was a god before him. At last he said, "How different you look, stranger! Your clothes, your complexion, your appearance—all have changed. You must be a god. Let me offer sacrifices to you. Spare us."

But Odysseus replied, "I am no god. I am your father. It's for my sake you've suffered so much violence and grief."

And he embraced his son affectionately. But Telemachus said at last, "Oh no, you are not my father Odysseus. Some god is tricking me, to make my grief harder to bear. No mortal could have plotted all this by himself. Only a god could change an old man into a young one. Surely, a moment ago you were old. Your clothes were rags. Now you're like a very god."

"O Telemachus," declared Odysseus, "don't be so amazed at the arrival of your father. I'm the only Odysseus that will ever come here. At last, after troubles aplenty, I have arrived home twenty years after setting forth. This change you noted was the work of Athena. It is easy for the gods to raise up a man or to bring him low."

At these words Telemachus threw his arms about his father, weeping happily. At last Telemachus said, "In what ship did you come here, dear father? Who brought you here? You didn't walk—that I know!"

"My son," replied Odysseus, "the seafaring Phaeacians brought me here. They gave me many gifts, which I have hidden in a cave. I have come here at Athena's suggestion to plan the slaughter of our enemies. Come; tell me about the suitors. How many are there? What kind of men are they? Give me full information so that I can judge whether we can handle them alone or with assistance."

Telemachus answered, "Father, I've always heard of your great glory. I knew that you were a warrior and a wise man. But what you have said amazes me beyond measure. To think that you feel two men might handle the whole group! There aren't ten suitors only or even twice ten. There are many more. There are fifty-two from Dulichium alone, with six servants. Twenty-four came from Samos. Twenty came from Zacynthus. Ithaca alone provided twelve good men. Besides all these there are the herald Medon and two skilled chefs. If we attack them all at once, I'm afraid you'll be sorry. If you can think of an assistant. please name him. We'll need help."

Odysseus answered with a twinkle in his eye, "Do

you think that Zeus and Athena will be good enough assistants, or will we need some others?"

"Well," replied Telemachus, "these are fine helpers, true. But they are the gods of our enemies, too!"

Odysseus replied, "They'll be in the thick of the fighting for us; don't worry. Go back to the palace and mix with those villainous scoundrels. Eumaeus will take me into the city dressed like an old beggar. If they show no respect for me, don't fret. Grin and bear it even if they drag me through the house by the feet! Try to convince them to be gentle. They won't, of course, for their day of doom is approaching.

"Listen to this, too. At the appropriate moment I'll nod to you. Then begin to hide all the arms that are around the palace. Make some excuse to the suitors that you are preserving the weapons away from the smoke. Say that you wouldn't like them to hurt each other if a chance quarrel should arise. But leave enough for the two of us.

"This is most important. Don't let anyone know that Odysseus has returned. Don't tell Laertes, Eumaeus, the servants, or even Penelope herself. We must set out to find who, among the servants, is faithful to our side."

"My father," replied Telemachus, "time will prove my spirit. I am no coward. But I don't think it will be profitable to test the loyalty of the servants one by one. Leave that till later."

And so they conversed.

In the meantime Telemachus's ship had reached the port of Ithaca. The men sent a herald to Penelope to tell her that Telemachus had come back safely. They wanted to set Penelope's mind at ease. The herald and the swineherd met on the way, both with the same message for Penelope.

When they came to the palace, the herald spoke out loud enough for the others to hear, "Queen Penelope, your son has come back."

Eumaeus drew Penelope aside, to give her the message from Telemachus. After he gave her the news, he left. But the suitors were angry. They came out of the palace and drew together nearby. One of the suitors, named Eurymachus, began to address the others.

"Friends, Telemachus has turned the tables boldly upon us. We thought he'd never come back alive. Let's send a ship to tell the men lying in ambush that the plot's off."

Scarcely had he finished when Amphinomus, turning on his seat, spied their friends' ship already in port. Laughing wryly, he addressed the others.

"Too late! The others are already back. Either some god has told them of Telemachus' escape, or else they saw his ship sailing by, out of reach."

All of the suitors went down to the vessel and helped beach it. Then they gathered for a meeting, letting no outsider join them, young or old.

Antinous, one of the leaders among the suitors, said,

"Curse it all. See how the gods have let this man escape his death. We kept lookouts constantly alert for sign of him. We never slept ashore, but cruised all night waiting for his vessel, to destroy it. Meanwhile he has come back safely. Well, let's not give up. He hasn't escaped yet. Let's plot his doom, for while he lives we'll get nowhere. He's by no means stupid, and, besides, the people like him.

"We must act before he gets his people together. For he'll be angry at our plot against his life. He'll tell the people how we planned his death. They won't like the news. They may even try to banish us. We'll act first. We'll kill him before he even gets back here. Then we'll split up all his wealth and divide it among us. Later we'll give the palace back to his mother and whoever marries her. If this seems too severe to you, then let's stop our living at his expense. Each one can then continue, from his own house, his attempts to woo Penelope."

A deathly silence fell over the group. At last Amphinomus spoke.

"Friends, I am not one who wishes to slay Telemachus. It is a terrible thing to kill one of noble race. Let's ask the counsel of the gods first. If Zeus himself advises it, then I'll kill him myself and urge the rest of you to be a party to the deed. If the gods say *no*, then I urge you to stop."

The group approved this counsel. They rose and went off again to the palace of Odysseus. But Penelope had her own ideas, clever woman that she was. She planned to appear before the suitors, for she had heard of the plot to kill her son. Accordingly, she went to the palace with her attendants. She stood before them veiled. Turning to Antinous, she scolded him by name.

"Antinous, you're a violent, scheming man. You have the reputation for wisdom. Not so! Madman, why do you plot the death of Telemachus? Don't you remember that when your father came here, a fugitive, Odysseus protected him from his enemies? Now you eat his food, woo his wife, and plan to slay his son. I urge you to stop and to persuade the others to stop, too."

Eurymachus answered her.

"Wise Penelope, don't worry. No one will lay a hand on Telemachus—at least not while I'm alive. I remember how well Odysseus treated me. For his sake Telemachus is dear to me. He need fear nothing from the suitors."

That is what he said, though actually he was plotting the death of Telemachus along with the others. Reassured, she went up to her rooms and cried herself to sleep for Odysseus.

In the evening the swineherd returned to Odysseus and his son. They were preparing a pig for supper. Athena had changed Odysseus once more into an old man, with rags for clothes. Thus Eumaeus did not know him as Odysseus. Telemachus spoke first.

"Back again, Eumaeus! What's new? Did the scoundrels come home from their attempted ambush? Or are they still out there waiting for me to sail by?"

"That I don't know," confessed Eumaeus. "I was in a hurry to get back here. But I do know that a messenger from the ship blurted out the news of your return in front of everybody. Just as I rounded the hill near the harbor I saw a ship coming in, loaded with armed men. Perhaps these were the suitors."

Telemachus smiled and caught his father's eye. After they did their chores, they had their supper and were soon sound asleep.

CHAPTER THIRTEEN

Odysseus Returns Home

In the morning Telemachus said to Eumaeus, "I am going to the city to see my mother. Bring the stranger to the city to beg a meal there. I can't carry the woes of all the world. I have enough of my own. If the stranger is angry, it will be too bad. I must speak plainly."

Odysseus broke in. "My friend, I'd rather not stay here anyway. The city is the best place for a beggar. Any charitable person will give me something. You go on. This man will take me to the city, as you wish, after the sun has climbed a little higher. For it's cold here mornings, and the city is a long way off, you say."

Telemachus went off, with plans for vengeance forming in his mind. At last he reached the palace and passed over the threshold. Nurse Eurycleia saw him first. Weeping, she went directly to him. All the other maids surrounded him joyfully. Penelope herself came from her rooms—beautiful to see. She threw her arms around her dear son tearfully. Kissing him she said, "You've come at last, my dear Telemachus. I thought I'd never see you again when you went off to Pylos against my wishes. What news have you for me?"

Telemachus replied, "Dear mother, do not make me

feel sorrowful all over again, even if I have escaped death. Pray to Zeus for vengeance. Meanwhile I'm going off to the market place. There I've an appointment with a stranger I met coming here. I told one of our men to take him home to entertain him."

She was impressed by his manner and went off to do as he asked. He left the palace, accompanied by his favorite hounds. Athena made him even more handsome and majestic to look at. The people admired him. The suitors gathered around him, flattering him even while they were plotting his death. He avoided the crowd as best he could. Soon one of his men came, leading Theoclymenus, the prophet, toward him.

Telemachus led the prophet to the palace, where they both washed and put on clean clothing. At the meal Penelope sat opposite them. At last she said, "Telemachus, I'm going to my room to lie down. Many a time I've cried myself to sleep yearning for Odysseus. You still haven't told me if you have news of your father."

"This is the whole story," replied Telemachus. "We went to Pylos first. No one there had any news of Odysseus. From Pylos I went to Sparta. Menelaus is king there. I met his wife, the famous Helen of Troy —the very Helen over whom the Trojan War was fought! He asked me why I'd come to Sparta.

"When I told him how things are back in Ithaca, Menelaus said, 'What cowards those suitors must be to try to steal the place of a strong man! Odysseus will slay them as a lion slays the kids. I hope when he returns he's the same Odysseus who wrestled one of the strongest of the Greeks—and won! Then the suitors will have a swift death and a bitter wedding. I do have this bit of news for you. I've heard that Odysseus has been trapped by the goddess Calypso, though he yearns to come home again.'

"That was all the news Menelaus could give me. So I left and sped back home here."

The prophet, who had listened to all this, declared, "Honored Penelope, wife of Odysseus, Menelaus does not know the whole truth. Listen to me. As Zeus is my witness, I believe that Odysseus is now here in Ithaca. I believe that he is at this very moment plotting the death of the suitors. When we left the ship, we were given a good omen. That is how I interpret it."

Penelope replied, "Ah, if this is true, then you'll benefit from your friendship with me. You'll know my gratitude."

During this conversation the suitors were enjoying themselves, throwing javelins and playing at quoits. Finally Medon, one of their favorite heralds, came out and said, "Come along, lads, you've all enjoyed yourselves. Now come inside for a feast. It's supper time."

In they went boisterously. And they sacrificed pigs and cattle and goats, and prepared their meal.

At the same time Odysseus and the swineherd were preparing to go to the city. Eumaeus turned to Odysseus and said, "Stranger, since you have your heart set on going to the city, you might as well go. I'd rather have you here with me. But I wouldn't want Telemachus to be angry with me. Come, then; let's go. The day is moving along. In the evening it'll be cold again."

Odysseus replied, "Yes, I know. Well, let's go. Please lend me a staff to lean on—if you have one. You've said the path is slippery."

He put on his old rags, and Eumaeus gave him a sturdy walking-stick. And so Eumaeus led his master to the city—looking like a weak old beggar with miserable garments. When they reached the outskirts of the city, they stopped for a moment at a beautiful fountain. While there, they were met by a man leading two goats, fat ones, as part of the supper for the suitors. His name was Melanthius. When he saw Odysseus and Eumaeus, Melanthius spoke scornfully. Odysseus could scarcely restrain himself.

"Well, well, well," Melanthius said, "one beggar leading another! Birds of a feather flock together, they always say. Where, my king of the pigs, are you leading this starved old beggar? The sight of him would destroy anyone's appetite! If he did an honest day's work, he might fatten out a bit. But he's the lazy kind that prefers begging. I'll tell you this: if he goes to the palace, he'll get a royal welcome. They'll wear out many footstools on his crown!"

As Melanthius passed, the fool kicked Odysseus, but the hero did not budge. Odysseus debated whether to kill him with a blow, or let him go. He restrained himself at last. Eumaeus, though, had something to say, as he prayed aloud.

"O nymphs of this fountain, bring back Odysseus! Then he'll get rid of all these boasters and insolent rascals."

But Melanthius replied, "Ye gods, how this vicious mongrel talks. Some day I'll take him off and sell him for profit elsewhere. I only wish that the suitors would kill Telemachus as surely as Odysseus lies under the sod somewhere."

The herder of goats left the two and went back to the palace, where he sat near Eurymachus, whom he loved particularly.

By this time Odysseus and Eumaeus had reached the palace, too. Inside a harpist had begun to entertain the suitors. Odysseus spoke to Eumaeus.

"Eumaeus, this palace of Odysseus' is truly magnificent. It would stand out even among other elaborate dwellings. I see that many men are feasting here. I detect the odor of good roast beef, and I hear a harpist inside."

"You've seen that readily enough," replied Eu-

He wagged his tail, but could not drag his body to his master.

maeus. "You're no fool. But let's decide what to do. Would you rather go first into the house, or have me lead the way? If you choose the latter, don't linger outside, for you'll be stoned for sure. Which would you prefer?"

"Perhaps you'd better go first," said Odysseus. "I'll wait here. Stones and blows are no novelty to me. I've had my share of blows in war and on sea. Let things happen as they will. But it's difficult to conceal a hungry stomach—stomachs cause too much trouble!"

As they spoke, Argus, Odysseus' dog, pricked up his ears. He had been a favorite of Odysseus' many years ago, before Odysseus had sailed to Troy. But after Odysseus had left, he had been neglected. He lay outside sorrowfully, flea-ridden and mangy. When he saw and heard Odysseus again, he wagged his tail, but could not drag his body to his master. Seeing him there, Odysseus wiped a tear away before Eumaeus could see it. At last he spoke.

"Eumaeus, it's a shame to see such a beautiful dog uncared for. Was he a good hunting dog, or a pampered house dog?"

Eumaeus replied, "This is the dog of a man who died far away. If he were as good as he was when Odysseus left, then you'd be amazed at his speed and stout heart. He wasn't afraid of anything. He was an excellent tracker, too. Now he's in a bad way. His master's dead. The women neglect him—as servants will when the master's no longer around."

Having said this, Eumaeus went into the house and approached the suitors. But death claimed poor Argus, at seeing his master again after twenty years.

Telemachus saw Eumaeus first and called out to him. He sat down near Telemachus and was served. Odysseus came in soon afterward, looking like a poor old beggar leaning upon a stick for support. He sat down on the threshold. Telemachus said to Eumaeus, handing him bread and meat, "Give these to the stranger. Tell him to circulate among the suitors to ask for charity. Pride has no place in a beggar."

Eumaeus did as he was instructed and said to Odysseus, "Stranger, Telemachus gives you this and orders you to go begging among the suitors."

Odysseus replied, "May Zeus keep Telemachus happy, and make him successful in everything he plans!"

And so he ate, while the harpist continued his playing. At the end of the meal the suitors became even noisier. Athena stood near Odysseus and whispered to him to go begging among the suitors, to see which were just and which unjust. He went begging among them, stretching his hand out like any beggar. Several of them gave him something in pity. They asked each other who he was and where he came from. Melanthius, the goatherd, spoke up.

"Listen a moment, suitors to Penelope. I've seen this stranger before. He came with the swineherd. But I don't know who he is or where he comes from."

As he finished Antinous began to scold Eumaeus. "Villainous swineherd, why did you bring this fellow here to the city? Haven't we enough wanderers and beggars here already? Aren't there enough people here eating up your master's wealth? Must you bring more?"

Eumaeus replied, "Antinous, you may be noble but you speak improperly. I didn't invite him to this island. After all, he is but a beggar. But you're always the cruelest of the lot towards the servants and me especially. However, I can endure it as long as Penelope and Telemachus are here."

Telemachus said to Eumaeus, "Be silent. Don't answer him. He always tries to anger us."

To Antinous he said, "You take as good care of me, Antinous, as a father does of his son! Now you're trying to teach me to send a stranger out of the house. May Zeus never allow this! Give him charity. I advise you to. But no, you'd rather eat than give."

Antinous replied, "Listen to our Telemachus speak! If all the suitors give the beggar as much as I do, we'll not see him for at least three months."

As he spoke, he lifted the footstool threateningly. But all the others did contribute something. On his way out, Odysseus paused near Antinous and said, "Give, friend. You are certainly not the worst of this group. You look the noblest; therefore, you should be more generous than the others. If you give, I'll sing your praises over the whole wide world. Once upon a time I was happy and wealthy, too. Then I used to give generously to all wanderers.

"Ah, yes. I had many servants and much wealth, but the gods sent me off to Egypt. There my men started killing and looting. That started all my trouble. Well, here I am—in a bad way indeed!"

Antinous replied, "Who sent us this pest? Get away from me or I'll give you another Egypt for your troubles. You're nothing but a dirty old beggar. These others foolishly give to you. They're generous—with somebody else's goods!"

Odysseus withdrew, saying, "Too bad! Your mind doesn't match your appearance. You wouldn't give your own servant a pinch of salt! There's plenty here, too."

This enraged Antinous. Looking sternly at Odysseus, he said, "You won't get away from here with a whole skin after that exhibition of insolence."

As he spoke, he picked up a footstool and threw it at Odysseus. It struck him on the shoulder, but Odysseus did not stumble. He merely moved silently away and shook his head. But he planned an evil fate for the suitors. He went back to the door, sat down, and spoke aloud.

"Listen, you suitors of a noble queen. I have something to say to you. A man is not bitter when he is struck defending his possessions. But Antinous hit me because of my hunger. If there are any gods and Furies on the side of poor men, then I hope he dies before he marries."

Antinous retorted, "Eat quietly, stranger, or get out. Otherwise you may be dragged through the house on your back or skinned alive."

But the other suitors objected. One of them said, "Antinous, that was unwise of you to strike the poor old wanderer. If there are gods in heaven, you may be punished. You know how the gods keep an eye on us mortals."

Antinous did not listen to their words. Telemachus worried for his father, that he might have been hurt by the blow. But he could not show his concern. Instead he brooded in silence.

Penelope, too, was shocked to hear of the treatment of the poor old man.

"May the gods destroy Antinous!" she exclaimed.

"If all our prayers were heard," declared one of the maids, "none of the suitors would live till morning."

"Nurse," said Penelope, "they're all hateful to me, plotters that they are! But I hate Antinous most of all. Some poor beggar is wandering through our halls. The others gave, but Antinous threw a footstool at him."

Having called the swineherd to her she said, "Eumaeus, tell the stranger to come here, so that I can talk to him. I must ask him whether he has any news of Odysseus. Perhaps he has even seen him, for he seems like a man who has traveled widely."

"My lady," replied Eumaeus, "if they'd only be quiet down there, the stranger could tell some wonderful stories. I had his company for three days and three nights, for he came to me first. He hasn't finished telling his troubles even yet! Ah, he's a great story-teller. I enjoyed his company. He says he's a friend of the master's family. He keeps saying that Odysseus is still alive near the people of the Thesprotians. He says the master's coming back soon weighted down with presents."

"Hurry, then," declared Penelope; "call him here. I want to speak to him. As for the others—let them have their fun. They should be enjoying themselves! Their goods lie untouched in their own homes. Here they're eating up all our wealth. And there's no one here—like Odysseus—to keep these enemies away. If Odysseus would only come, he'd soon have revenge on them with the help of his son."

As she spoke, Telemachus sneezed loudly. Penelope laughed and said, "Hurry. Don't you see that my son has sneezed at my words. They must be true. Death will come to all the suitors; not one will escape. I'll tell you this: if he's telling the truth, I'll reward him generously."

Eumaeus went back to the hall and addressed Odysseus.

"Stranger, our queen would like to speak with you. She is eager to ask for news of her husband. If you tell the truth, she'll reward you with fine clothes and other things. And you'll be able to go begging in style!"

Odysseus replied, "I'll tell her the truth, don't you

worry. Both Odysseus and I have endured the same hardships. But I fear this mob of insolent men. Just a moment ago this man struck me as I went innocently enough through the house. Tell the lady, eager though she is, to wait in her rooms until sunset. Then she can ask me all about her husband. I am not now dressed decently, as you can see."

When Eumaeus returned, Penelope declared, "Oh, you don't have him with you, Eumaeus! Why not? Is he afraid of bad treatment, or is he merely shy?"

Eumaeus replied, "He's sensible. He asks you to wait until sunset. It is a better idea for you to speak to him alone."

Then Eumaeus went back to the hall and singled out Telemachus. "I am off to guard the swine, sir. Watch everything here. Take care of yourself. Don't get into trouble. Many of these Greeks are plotting your death —may Zeus kill them all."

Telemachus answered, "Very well, Eumaeus. But come back here in the morning."

CHAPTER FOURTEEN

Odysseus and the Beggar

By this time it was afternoon. The feasters were still enjoying themselves when another beggar appeared. This fellow, called Irus by the suitors, was noted for his hungry stomach. When he saw Odysseus, Irus tried to drive him from his own house, saying, "Get away from here, old man, or I'll have to drag you out by the leg. Can't you see that they're all winking at me to throw you out? But I'm ashamed to do it. Now go, or else we may have to come to blows!"

Looking sternly at the beggar, Odysseus declared, "I don't harm you and I don't speak harm of you. Get all you can from the others. I don't grudge it to you, no matter how much you get. There's room here for both of us. You shouldn't begrudge anything to me, either. You seem to be a wanderer like me. But I warn you: don't arouse me to fight with you. I might get angry and bloody you up a bit, to get some quiet tomorrow. I don't think you'd come again to this house."

Irus was furious.

"Ye gods," he cried, "how this greedy old fellow prattles. He's like an old washerwoman. I ought to give him a good right and a left, and knock all his teeth out. Well, on your guard then. Let the others watch

148

us. How do you expect to stand up against a younger man?"

They glared angrily at each other and squared for the fight. Antinous, with a hearty laugh, cried out:

"This is excellent, friends. We've never had such fun before. The gods are treating us well today. If these gentlemen want to fight each other, we'll help them along."

The others all got up, laughing, too. They formed a ring around the two wretchedly dressed beggars. Antinous cried out again.

"Wait a moment, noble suitors, while I speak to these boxers. We have a good supper on the fire. The winner will eat well. Besides he'll have the privilege of always eating with us and being the only beggar allowed to ask charity of us."

They thought this a good plan, but Odysseus had plans, too.

"Friends," he declared, "an old man, worn out and weary, cannot stand up to a younger man. But my cursed stomach urges me on to take a beating. Well, come, all of you must swear an oath that you will not take Irus's part and strike me during the fight."

They agreed to play fair. Then Telemachus broke in.

"Don't worry, stranger. If you win, you need fear none of the Greeks here. If anyone strikes you, he'll have all the rest of us to contend with. I'm sure those great kings Eurymachus and Antinous will agree with me."

All approved his speech. Odysseus tucked up his rags about his middle and revealed his powerful build. His broad shoulders and strong arms stood out clearly and all the suitors were amazed. One of the suitors turned to his neighbor and said, "Poor Irus! This fellow is stronger than he at first seemed!"

Irus was frightened, too, and he shook as the attendants prepared him for the fight. Antinous noted this and said, "Well, my boasting friend, you'll wish you had never been born if you shake at sight of this weary old man. I promise you this: if he wins over you, I'll ship you off to old King Echetus, who'll cut off your nose and ears and feed the rest of you to the dogs."

Irus shook even more at these words. The attendants led the two fighters to a cleared space. The two men squared off for the fight. For the moment Odysseus couldn't make up his mind whether to kill Irus at one blow or merely stun him. Irus made the first thrust, driving a blow that struck Odysseus on the shoulder. But Odysseus hammered a blow that struck Irus on the neck just below the ear. The blow shattered all the bones and sent the blood rushing through Irus' mouth. Irus fell groaning in the dust, gnashing his teeth and kicking the earth in agony.

The suitors nearly died of laughing at the sight. But Odysseus took Irus by the leg and dragged him out of the house into the yard. He propped him up against the fence, put the stick in his hand, and said,

*Odysseus hammered a blow that struck Irus on the neck
just below the ear.*

"Sit here and keep the pigs and dogs away. Contemptible wretch, don't try to be king of the beggars or something worse may happen to you!"

Odysseus threw the beggar's miserable belongings to him and went back to the hall. The suitors were still laughing. One of them said, "May Zeus grant you all your wishes, stranger. You've got rid of this hungry beggar at last. We'll send that fellow over to King Echetus, to be sure."

Odysseus was happy at this excellent beginning. Amphinomus, one of the suitors, gave him some bread, saying, "Stranger, I hope you prosper finally, though you are now in a bad way."

Odysseus replied to him, "Amphinomus, you look to me like a wise man. Therefore I am giving you advice. I hope for your sake you'll listen. I was once prosperous and foolish. I trusted in violence and power above all else. Now look at me! This is a warning to all lawless men. I see many men here wasting another man's possessions and annoying his wife. The man will probably come back—and not long from now! I hope you'll leave here and go home secretly, for when the man returns, I don't believe any suitor will be left alive."

Amphinomus was touched at these words, and he thought about them. But he did nothing. He went back among the suitors, and so he was among those who later met their death in the halls of Odysseus.

Meanwhile Athena put it in Penelope's mind to go

once again before the suitors. Athena had two reasons: to flutter the hearts of the suitors, and to make Penelope that much more desirable to her husband and her son. Accordingly, Penelope said to her maid, "I don't know why, but I have a strange notion. I think I'll go before the suitors, hateful though they are. I want to warn Telemachus not to mingle with the suitors, who flatter while they scheme."

"A good idea," declared the maid, "but come; wash the tears off your face first. Don't conceal your beauty."

"Beauty!" exclaimed Penelope. "Since Odysseus left, I have lost my beauty. Tell two of the other servants to come with me among the men. I don't wish to go alone."

The woman went off to tell them, and Athena caused Penelope to fall asleep. The goddess made Penelope more beautiful to look at than ever. When the girls arrived, Penelope awakened and said, "I must have fallen asleep. I wish I could sleep and never wake up again. I miss Odysseus so."

She rose and went down to the hall, followed by the two handmaidens. Standing between the girls, she leaned against a pillar. The men were stunned at her beauty. But she turned to her son and said, "Telemachus, your mind and courage are not what they used to be. How brilliant you were as a child, how tactful! Now that you are a man you no longer use good judgment. Why have you allowed this poor stranger to be treated so shabbily? What if a guest should be injured through this kind of mistreatment? You'd be disgraced in the eyes of men."

Telemachus replied, "Mother, I'm not surprised at your anger. But I do know the difference between right and wrong, though I am young. I cannot, though, always think of the right thing to do. These men crowding about keep me confused, plotters that they are. I have no one to help me, you know.

"That battle between Irus and the stranger did not go as the suitors wished. The stranger proved the better man. I pray to Zeus that all these grasping suitors will be overcome here in the palace just as Irus was. Irus lies outside, like a drunken man. He cannot even rise to go home."

Eurymachus interrupted the conversation, saying, "Penelope, it's a lucky thing all the Greeks cannot see you today. There'd be even more suitors about—you are so beautiful."

"Eurymachus," replied Penelope, "my beauty was lost when the Greeks left for Troy with my husband Odysseus. If he'd only return, then my good name might once again be restored. But now I waste away with grief. When he left me, he took me by the wrist and said, 'Dear lady, many of the Greeks will never see their homelands again. The Trojans are excellent fighters, men who can draw the bow and ride a steed with skill. I cannot know whether Zeus will let me return, or whether I'll die on the plains of Troy. I leave

everything here in your care. Watch over my father
and my mother even more than now. When your son
is old enough to have a beard, then marry again and
leave him this palace for himself.'

"Now all is turning out as he said. A day will come
when I'll be forced to marry against my will. But I
am humiliated by what has happened. Usually suitors
wooing a rich man's daughter bring gifts: oxen and
sheep, as a feast for the girl's friends. They don't eat
up the wealth of others."

Odysseus was delighted at her speech. He saw how
she coaxed gifts from them, soothing them while planning other things.

Antinous turned to Penelope and said, "Penelope,
you are right of course. Accept all gifts that we arrange to send you. But don't expect to be rid of us
until you marry the one you consider best among us."

The other suitors applauded his words and sent
men to get gifts for Penelope. When they had all been
collected and while her women were carrying them
off, Penelope returned to her own room.

The young men amused themselves in singing and
dancing until evening. When the lights were lit, Odysseus turned to the serving girls who were still there
and said, "Girls, go to your mistress and stay with
her. I'll serve these men and take care of their needs.
I can last till morning if they need me."

The girls laughed merrily at his words, but Melantho scolded him. She had been brought up almost as

Penelope's own daughter, but she had no love for Penelope. In fact, she was in love with one of the suitors, Eurymachus.

"You old vagabond," she said, "you must be soft in the head! You ought to be off sleeping at the blacksmith's instead of staying here among these gentlemen. You speak as boldly as can be. The wine must have gone to your head, or perhaps you always talk such nonsense. Are you boasting at your defeat of Irus? Watch out or a stronger Irus will give you a sound beating and send you out soaked with your own blood."

"Hussy," exclaimed Odysseus angrily, "I'll tell Telemachus what you've said and he'll cut you up into little pieces."

The girls went off shrieking in terror, for they thought he meant his words. Odysseus turned again to the suitors and brooded over his plans. Athena could not let the proud suitors stop insulting Odysseus, for she wanted to make him even angrier at them. Eurymachus began the scoffing. He soon had the suitors roaring with laughter.

"Listen, suitors of a noble queen; I have some things to say to you. This beggar probably comes to us through the will of some god. As a matter of fact the divine fire seems to be shining out of the top of his head, for there's no hair there to stop it!"

Then he turned to Odysseus. "Stranger, would you be willing to take a job if I offered you one? I need somebody for clearing rocks from the fields and planting trees. I'd keep you on for a year and feed you well. Ah no, I think you're not too anxious to work. You'd rather beg to feed your belly."

"Eurymachus," replied Odysseus, "I wish we could have a contest in the spring. You could take a sickle and I'd take one. We'd soon see who is the better man. Or perhaps we could have a plowing contest. Then you could watch me cut the furrows. Or if war arose and I had spears, shield and helmet, you'd find me among the first fighters. Then you wouldn't poke fun at me for my hunger.

"You have insulted me much, you bully! You consider yourself a leader among men because you associate with these rabble. If Odysseus should come back, these gates—wide though they are—would be too narrow for you to escape through."

Eurymachus in rage said, "You rascal! I'll fix you for your brazen speech. You just have no respect. You're either soaked with wine or a constant boaster. Are you still inflated over your defeat of Irus?"

As he spoke he picked up a stool, but Odysseus ducked behind the knees of Amphinomus. The stool struck the wine-bearer on the arm. Down fell the bowl, resounding on the ground. The poor fellow fell groaning. Then there was an uproar. One of the suitors said to a friend, "I would to heaven the stranger had died before he ever came here. Then he would not have

As he spoke he picked up a stool.

caused this tumult. Now we are fighting over a miserable beggar, spoiling our banquet."

Telemachus cried out, "Sirs, you are mad! You cannot eat and drink quietly. You'd better go home to your rest. I am not chasing you away, mind you."

The suitors bit their lips, surprised at the boldness of Telemachus. Amphinomus said, at last, "Friends, he is right. No one can object to what he has said. Stop insulting the stranger. Come; let us drink a toast and then go home to bed. Let us leave the stranger to Telemachus to take care of. He came to his house, after all."

The others were pleased at these words. After they drank the toast, they left the palace and went home.

CHAPTER FIFTEEN

The Nurse Recognizes Odysseus

Odysseus was left alone with Telemachus. He turned to his son, saying, "Telemachus, you'd better put all the arms safely away. Put the suitors off with some excuse when they ask about the weapons. Say you are putting them away from the smoke, which tarnishes them. Or tell them that you wouldn't want them to hurt themselves in a drunken quarrel."

Telemachus set to work at once. On the way out he called to the nurse Eurycleia.

"Nurse, come now; lock up for the night. I am going to store my father's armor away. I don't want the smoke to tarnish it."

"My child," replied Eurycleia, "I wish you'd take care of your house and all that's in it. Ah well, who is to carry the light for you?"

Telemachus said, "This stranger. I'll keep him working even if he does come from a long way off."

The nurse shut the gates, while Odysseus and his son hurried off to their job. As they gathered the arms and stored them away, Athena went before them, holding a golden lamp.

Telemachus was amazed and said, "Father, I am seeing some miracle. Everything looks as if it were lit with a golden fire. Is some god among us?"

"Hush," said Odysseus, "ask no questions. This is

162

the way of the immortal gods. Go and lie down. I'll stay here. I want to speak with your mother."

Telemachus went out and Odysseus waited. Soon Penelope entered the room, beautiful as the golden moon-goddess, Artemis. She sat down and waited as the maidens removed the remnants of the night's feast. Once again Melantho, her serving maid, scolded Odysseus.

"Stranger, are you still here to annoy us? Still spying on us? Why don't you go away and be grateful for the meal you've had? Shall we chase you with a torch?"

"Brazen woman," said Odysseus sternly, "why do you attack me so bitterly? Is it because I am dressed poorly? Because I am forced to beg? I was once wealthy and powerful. Then I often gave to a wanderer, no matter who he was, when he came to me in need. Now the gods have brought me to this. But you, woman, ought to watch out. Some day you may lose your beauty and the fine place you have here. Perhaps your mistress will become angry with you, or maybe Odysseus will return. There is still hope of that. But even if he has perished, he still has his son Telemachus to take revenge upon those women who act shamelessly."

Penelope scolded the woman too, saying, "You're an impudent girl, and you'll suffer from your boldness. You knew perfectly well that I sent for the stranger to ask about my husband."

She invited Odysseus to sit down before her and she began to question him.

"Stranger," she said, "let me ask first who you are and where you came from. Where are your parents and your city?"

"Lady," replied Odysseus thoughtfully, "no one can find fault with you. Your fame reaches heaven itself. Please ask me anything else, but don't ask about my home and my parents. For this will bring all my troubles to mind again. I dislike moping about mournfully in someone else's house."

Penelope said, "Stranger, I lost all excellence when my husband left for Troy with the other Greeks. If he came home, then I'd truly have a good name again. Now I have many problems. All the leaders of the neighboring islands have come here against my will to woo me. Thus I am bitter and stay by myself, yearning for Odysseus. They try to hurry the marriage, but I have a trick or two. Some god inspired me to weave a large robe on my loom.

"I said to these suitors, 'Youths, now that Odysseus has died, you are here urging me to marry again. But I must finish this robe first as a burial-robe for Laertes, Odysseus' father, when he ends his days on earth. I wouldn't want people to talk because I do not have a decent burial garment for my dear father-in-law.' They were persuaded by my words.

"So, during the day, I wove the cloth, but in the night I unraveled the threads again. For three years

I was able to trick them in this way. However, in the fourth year they discovered my secret through the treachery of my own servants. How they scolded me! So I had to finish the robe against my will. Now matters have come to a head. I cannot escape marriage, and I have no other plan. Even my parents are urging me to marry. My son is furious to see the suitors eating up all his wealth, for he's a man now and would like to manage the place. Well, so much for me. Now tell me about you, where you came from. You certainly weren't born of an oak or a rock!"

Odysseus replied, "Honored wife of Odysseus, won't you stop asking about my people? Well, I will tell you and so be reminded of my troubles. That's the way it is when a man's a wanderer as I am. All right, then, here's the tale.

"In the middle of the sea lies a dark and beautiful island called Crete. The island holds numerous men and ninety cities. Different dialects and languages are plentiful. On the island is a large city, Cnossus. There Minos was king, who talked with Zeus. He was my father's own father. My brother went off to the Trojan War.

"In Crete I met Odysseus and gave him many gifts. For Odysseus stopped off in Crete on his way to Troy. He and his Greeks stayed in Crete for twelve days. On the thirteenth day the wind fell and they set off again."

He paused a moment in spinning his yarn, for he

loved storytelling and he was a master at it. But poor Penelope began to cry. Odysseus felt sorry for her then and had to restrain himself from weeping. At last she spoke.

"Stranger, I'm going to test you to see whether you really did entertain my husband as you say. What clothing was he wearing? What kind of person was he? What were his men like?"

"My lady," replied Odysseus, "it's difficult to remember after so many years. After all, it is twenty years since he left Ithaca and stopped at Crete. Well, I'll tell you, as I seem to recall.

"Odysseus wore a purple woolen cloak, doubled over. He had on it a golden clasp with two fastenings. The design of the clasp was a dog holding a spotted fawn. It was so realistic that everyone was amazed at it. I remember another garment he wore, a tunic which glistened like the skin of an onion. Many women admired it. Of course, I don't know whether Odysseus left here with those clothes, or whether they were given to him on the way. For everybody loved Odysseus. I gave him many gifts myself and sent him along. Oh yes, there was a herald who followed him, a man a little older than he. His name was Eurybates. Odysseus loved the fellow above all the others."

These words merely increased the flood of tears, for they were, naturally enough, the truth! At last she spoke.

"A moment ago, stranger, you were an object of

pity. Now you are dear to me, beyond all measure. I myself gave him the clothes you describe. It was I who put the shining clasp on them for ornament. Now I'm afraid I'll never see him again. Curse the day he ever left for Troy!"

Odysseus answered, "Noble wife of Odysseus, don't waste away in mourning for your husband. True, I can understand your feelings. Any woman feels sorrowful when she has lost her husband—even a husband inferior to that god-like Odysseus. Stop your crying, though, and listen to me. I'm going to tell you the truth about Odysseus. I have some very recent news of him. He is alive, among the Thesprotians. He is coming back with treasure, though he has lost all his comrades and ships. It seems that the Sun God and Zeus were angry with him, for his comrades slaughtered the Sun's cattle. All the men drowned.

"Odysseus was saved, for he held onto the keel of the ship and landed among the Phaeacians. They honored him and gave him many gifts. They offered to convoy him home. If they had, Odysseus would be here by now. But he thought it best to go home by the land route and gather more before he returned. You know how Odysseus is always on the alert in business matters. No one can match that fellow!

"The king of the Thesprotians swore to me personally that the ship was ready to sail that would bring Odysseus back to Ithaca. I left before Odysseus sailed, but I saw some of the wealth he had gathered. They'd keep a man's family rich for ten generations. The king said that Odysseus was off to Dodona for advice before leaving for home. For Odysseus did not know whether to return in secret or openly. So you see Odysseus is safe and will be home soon. I will make this pledge to you. Let Zeus be my witness. All this will happen this year before another month is out!"

Then the faithful Penelope replied, "I hope with all my heart that you are speaking the truth, stranger. Then you'll be rewarded for your words. But I feel that it's not to be. My heart tells me that Odysseus will never come home again. Ah, there's nobody here now like Odysseus. There was a man—always ready to receive strangers and to send them on, honored. . . .

"Well, then, my handmaidens, wash the stranger and prepare his bed, so that he may take breakfast with Telemachus. If any of the men is cruel toward you, it will be too bad for him. He'll have to leave at once. How else can I honor you?"

Odysseus declared, "Honored wife of Odysseus, I have no use for cloaks and beautiful rugs ever since I left Crete long ago. I'll continue to lie as I have lain many sleepless nights on a rough bed waiting for dawn. Nor can I allow any of the women to wash me, unless there is an old woman here, wise and tolerant of suffering. She may bathe my feet—no other."

"Dear guest," replied Penelope, "no stranger has ever come here wiser than you! You have spoken so sensibly. I do have such an old woman, who cared for

This was the scar that the old woman recognized.

poor Odysseus as a child. Indeed she took him under her wing when he was but an infant. She is old and feeble, but she will bathe your feet.

"Come here, Eurycleia, and wash one who is the same age as your master. No doubt Odysseus now has hands as old and wrinkled, for misfortune ages men."

The old woman heard and covered her face. Wiping away the tears she said, "Alas, what can I do for my poor master? Zeus must hate him above all men. No man ever sacrificed so freely to the gods, and yet he's the one whose return was not granted. All he asked for was a quiet old age—in peace to bring up his noble son.

"I suppose the women in other lands make fun of him as the ones here do of you, stranger. I don't blame you for refusing to take their insults. Well, I'm willing to do as Penelope asks. I'll bathe your feet for her sake and for yours. I must say this, though. Many poor strangers have already wandered into the palace. But I've never seen anyone who looks as much like Odysseus, or even talks as much like him, as you do!"

"Yes, indeed," replied Odysseus; "many people who have seen both of us say that we do look very much alike. You have sharp eyes."

The old woman took a kettleful of hot water and poured cold into it. Odysseus turned away to a darker corner away from the light. He suddenly remembered that he had a scar which she would recognize. And she did! Going up to him, she began to bathe his feet,

when her eyes fell upon the telltale scar. Long ago in
a boar hunt Odysseus had charged a wild boar. The
boar had sidestepped the rush, and struck Odysseus
above the knee. The tusk had just missed the bone.
Despite his wound Odysseus had struck the boar
through the right shoulder and killed him. His companions had bathed the wound and bound it up. But a
scar always remained.

This was the scar that the old woman recognized.
She let the leg fall in her surprise, and the water
spilled all over. Joy and grief filled her heart at once.
Her eyes filled with tears. Her warm voice was choked
with emotion. She spoke to Odysseus shakily.

"Certainly, my dear child, you are Odysseus. And
to think that I didn't know you until I saw the scar!"

She turned and spoke to Penelope, wishing to break
the news at once. But she could not see her, for Athena
prevented it. Odysseus drew Eurycleia nearer to him.

"Nurse, do you want to be the death of me? You
took care of me like a mother. After twenty years
I've returned. Since you did recognize me, don't tell a
soul. Don't let anyone else in the palace know of my
return. If you speak, I'll kill you along with the other
traitors in the household—even if you are my nurse."

Eurycleia replied, "Dear child, what nonsense are
you talking? You know my mind. You know that I
will not tell. Now I'll promise you something. If Zeus
allows you to destroy the suitors, then I'll tell the

names of all who are traitors and all who are innocent among the women servants here."

Odysseus replied, "That won't be necessary, nurse.
I can tell which are faithful. I've been keeping my
eyes open. But keep absolutely quiet."

Then Penelope went over to the two and said,
"Stranger, let me ask you for advice. Shall I stay here
with my son and guard my property and my house,
faithful to my husband? Or should I marry the best
among these suitors? As long as my son was a child,
I did not have to think of marrying again. But now
he's a man. I suppose he's eager for me to leave the
house. As it is, the suitors are consuming all his goods,
his inheritance.

"I had a dream. Perhaps you can explain it. There
are twenty geese around the place which come in from
the pond for their daily grain. In my dream I saw a
great eagle drop from the mountain heights upon them,
killing all of them. They lay around the palace in dis-
order, but the eagle soared off to the heights again. I
cried aloud and the women around me set up a wailing.

"But the eagle came back and said with the voice
of a human being, 'Don't worry, Penelope; this is
more than a dream. It is a prophecy. The geese are
the suitors. I am your husband, the eagle which slew
the geese. And so it will come about.' I awakened and
looked out. The geese were still there, eating their
grain in the usual feeding station."

Odysseus replied, "The dream can be explained in no other way. Of course, things will happen as foretold. Odysseus will come and slay all the suitors— every one."

"Stranger," answered wise Penelope, "dreams are uncertain things at best. They tell of doubtful matters. They don't always turn out. There are two gates through which dreams pass—the gates of horn and the gates of ivory. The dreams which come through the gates of ivory are deceptive. Their promises are not fulfilled. Those which come through the gates of horn are true. I'm afraid this dream did not come through the gates of horn. That would be too wonderful for my son and me!

"I'll tell you something else, though. Today is the hateful day when I leave my husband's house. For I am about to propose a contest. Whoever most easily bends the great bow of Odysseus and shoots an arrow through the target of twelve axe-heads wins me for a wife. I'll cast in my lot with him and leave this house which I entered as a bride. I'll often remember it with sadness."

"Good," replied Odysseus. "Don't put off the contest any longer. Cunning Odysseus will get here before they do, to stretch the bow and shoot the arrow through the target."

"My guest," declared Penelope, "if you'd be willing to sit beside me in the palace entertaining me, I'd never want to sleep. But all of us do need sleep. I'm going to my room upstairs to lie down. Meanwhile you can sleep down here, either on the ground or on a bed they prepare for you."

Then Penelope went upstairs and lay down, crying herself to sleep.

CHAPTER SIXTEEN

Zeus Sends an Omen

Odysseus prepared his bed, and one of the hand-maidens covered him. While he lay awake planning the destruction of the suitors, he could hear the giggling of the women servants as they left to see the suitors. He was furious, and debated whether to rush in and kill them now, or to keep back vengeance a while longer. At last he said to himself grimly, "Grin and bear it. You were once more badly off in the Cyclops' cave. You kept your counsel even when the Cyclops was devouring your comrades. You waited until your trickery got you out. Wait now!"

So he scolded himself for his impatience. He was restless, though, and tossed from side to side. In this anxious state Athena appeared to him and said, "Why are you still awake, poor fellow? You are in your own house. Your wife is safe upstairs. You have a son that any man would be proud to call his own."

"Indeed, goddess," replied Odysseus, "you have told the truth. Yet I can't sleep for thinking. How can I slay these suitors while they always stay together in great numbers? Besides, if I do slay them with your permission and Zeus's, how can I find refuge from their families? Surely a feud will follow. What about these problems?"

"You're a hard one to please," exclaimed Athena. "People follow the counsels of poor weak *mortals.* Here I am a *goddess,* who watches over you in all your troubles, and you are in doubt whether to follow my advice. I tell you this plainly. Even if fifty bands of such men surrounded you, you'd win out in the end. Come, now. Get some sleep. To stay awake all night is foolish. You'll soon be freed of your misfortunes."

While she spoke, he began to doze. Soon he was sound asleep, and Athena returned to Olympus. But poor Penelope awakened again. She prayed aloud to the goddess Artemis.

"O Artemis, noble daughter of Zeus, I wish you would slay me on the spot. If only I could see Odysseus once more, I'd be willing to die. I cannot stand the thought of being married to a lesser man. One can withstand sorrow if only sleep comes at night. But the gods have made even my dreams a source of sorrow. In my sleep I saw Odysseus once more looking as he did when he sailed off to Troy. I was happy once again, for I thought it was no dream but reality."

Morning came and Odysseus heard her weeping. Half asleep, he seemed to see that she knew him. He thought she was standing at his side. But then he awakened fully and put aside his rough bed. Next he carried the ox-hide out of doors and lifted his hands to Zeus.

"Father Zeus, it has been your will to bring me at last over sea and land to my own country. Till now you have put me through many trials, and I wonder whether at last I have your favor. Let one of those now awakening in the house speak an omen for me. And give me another sign outdoors, too."

As he prayed, Zeus heard him. He thundered in answer, and Odysseus was glad. A woman nearby, who was indoors grinding barley and wheat, spoke the omen Odysseus asked for. She stopped her work wearily and said, "Father Zeus, ruler of gods and men, you have sent forth a thunderclap from a cloudless sky. You are showing this as a sign to someone. Please fulfil a prayer for me, too. May this be the last time the suitors eat their fill in the house of Odysseus. May this be the last time I have to wear myself out grinding meal for them. May this be their last meal!"

Odysseus was glad to hear this omen. Now he was certain he would be revenged on the suitors.

Inside the house everything was bustling. The servants had lit the fires. Telemachus arose and went to the threshold. Singling out Eurycleia, he declared, "Nurse, have you taken good care of the stranger with food and bed? Or does he lie where he can, uncared for? You know mother. Sometimes she foolishly honors those who speak glibly, while neglecting visitors of solid worth."

Eurycleia replied, "There's no one to blame her. The stranger drank his wine and ate his fill. When bedtime came, Penelope told the handmaidens to prepare a bed for him, but he preferred to lie down on a rough oxhide and skins of sheep. We put a cloak over him and left him."

After he left, Eurycleia spoke to the maids.

"Hurry, girls, off to your jobs. Some of you sweep out the place and sprinkle it. Others lay the purple rugs on the seats. Clear off all the tables and wash all the dishes. Go to the fountain for water and bring it quickly. The suitors don't stay away long when there's food aplenty here."

They all busied themselves with their tasks. While they were working, Eumaeus arrived with three of his best fat pigs. Seeing Odysseus he said, "Well, stranger, do the Greeks give you any more respect, or do they still dishonor you as before?"

Odysseus replied, "Eumaeus, I wish the gods would avenge the suitors' insolence. They go on their way acting shamelessly."

While they were talking, Melanthius, the goatherd, came by, bringing his best goats for the feast. After the animals were tethered, he turned to Odysseus insultingly and said, "Are you still here, stranger, being an annoyance to all the people here? Why don't you go away? If you stay on much longer, we'll have to come to blows, for you're a shameless beggar. Other Greeks are feasting. Go to them."

Odysseus gritted his teeth and refrained from replying. But he silently plotted his revenge. When Melanthius left, Philoetius came with additional animals. He saw Eumaeus and went over to him.

"What stranger is this, swineherd, who has come here so recently? What nationality is he? Where does he come from? Poor fellow, he has the bearing of a king. But the gods do inflict troubles upon wanderers, when they pile sorrows even upon kings."

Standing near Odysseus, Philoetius shook his hand and said, "Greetings, and welcome to you. I hope you find happiness at last, though you're now weighed down with troubles. O Zeus, you are the most destructive of all the gods. You have no pity for the very men you have produced. You give them full measure of sorrow and trouble!

"How I broke into a sweat when I saw this stranger and thought how Odysseus might be at this very moment. How I wept when I thought of my dear master. Perhaps even at this very minute he is wandering among other people, in rags as is this stranger—if he is alive at all! If he is dead, here's a sigh for good Odysseus who set me to watch over his cattle when I was still a boy. How those cattle have increased! Now others are here forcing me to bring these cattle in for their feasts. These men don't give a fig for the son, nor do they fear the gods' vengeance either. They are breaking their necks in their haste to split up the possessions of the long-absent Odysseus.

"I keep thinking of this: it is certainly wicked, while the son is alive, to take all these cattle off to another master far away. But it is almost unbearable to stay here guarding these cattle, watching them being destroyed by a gang of villains. I'd have fled long ago with the cattle to another master if I didn't think of poor Odysseus. I still hope that he may come, poor soul, and send these suitors to their death."

Odysseus replied, "Herdsman, you talk like a man of sense and understanding. Since I think you have intelligence, I'll tell you this, and I'll swear an oath on it. Let Zeus be my witness: Odysseus will surely come home while you are here. If you wish, you will see the death of the suitors who riot here."

"Stranger," answered the herdsman, "I hope Zeus brings this about. If he does, you'll know my gratitude."

While they were talking together, the suitors were planning a new way to get rid of Telemachus. But as they conspired, a bird flew on their left hand—the unlucky side. Amphinomus turned to the rest and said, "Friends, this plan for the death of Telemachus will not work. Let's drop it for now, and go to the feast."

They agreed to the advice of Amphinomus and went into the palace. Telemachus seated Odysseus near himself and said aloud, "Stay here and drink wine among the others. I'll guard you from the blows and insults of the suitors. This is not a public house *yet*. It still belongs to me through Odysseus. As for you, suitors, don't offend this man, or there'll be trouble."

The suitors bit their lips at his words and were

amazed at the boldness of Telemachus. Antinous quieted them, saying, "Put up with the language, men, though he speaks so boldly. If Zeus hadn't just given us a warning not to kill him now, we'd have been rid of him and his talking."

Telemachus pretended not to notice. But Athena did not allow the suitors to stop their insolent remarks, for she wished to enrage Odysseus still more. Among the suitors there was a lawless rascal called Ctesippus, a man from Samos. He addressed the suitors.

"Listen a moment, good suitors, to what I have to say. Strangers have always been entitled to a fair share. It isn't fair to make a poor old guest sorrowful. So I am going to give him a present; then he can give a tip to the servants for their service."

As he finished, he picked up an ox's hoof nearby. He threw it quickly at Odysseus, but Odysseus avoided it neatly with a turn of his head. He smiled bitterly at the deed. Telemachus scolded Ctesippus, saying, "It's a lucky thing, Ctesippus, you didn't hit the stranger. If you had, I'd have run you through with the spear, and your father would be more concerned about burying you than marrying you.

"I am warning all of you now. I'll not have such behavior in my house. I'm a man now and not a child. I've had to put up with your actions, because you are so many. But enough of this. If you wish to kill me, I'd prefer it to seeing you forever acting like uncivilized barbarians."

The suitors fell silent. At last Agelaus, one of the suitors, said, "Friends, no one can take offense at these words. Stop insulting the stranger and any of the servants of Odysseus. I would like to say this to Telemachus, though. As long as all of us expected, in our hearts, that Odysseus would return, then we could not blame Penelope for not marrying again. It's now obvious he'll never come back. Go to your mother, Telemachus, and tell her to select the best man as her husband. Then you can manage all your own property in peace, while she goes off with another."

Telemachus replied, "No, by Zeus, Agelaus, I don't delay my mother's marriage. I've been asking her to marry the one she considers best, but I can't turn her out if she refuses, now can I?"

Athena set the suitors to laughing at this, but in the midst of the loud laughter the prophet Theoclymenus, who had come with Telemachus, broke in.

"Alas, you fools! Why are you laughing? What is happening to you? Your hands, your faces, your knees are wrapped in darkness. There is a moaning in the air. Your cheeks are wet with tears. And look! the walls are splashed with blood. The hall is filled with phantoms—hurrying down to Hades and the darkness. The sun is gone. A thick fog has spread over all of you."

The suitors merely laughed more at his words. One of them said, "This man is in a daze. He doesn't know our ways. Send him out of the house, lads."

Theoclymenus replied, "I'll go, my friends, and glad to be out, too. For I have a feeling that death is coming soon to all of you who sit here in the house of Odysseus."

After he left, another suitor said scornfully, "Telemachus, there's nobody who has worse guests than you do. This fellow here is a begging loafer looking only for a meal—completely useless. And the fellow that left: wasn't he ready to make prophecies and annoy us! I have a good idea. Let's get the two of them together and sell them to the Sicilians for slaves. They may bring a good price!"

Telemachus disregarded the words, looking silently toward his father, waiting for the signal to slay the suitors.

Penelope entered and sat opposite them. She had heard the suitors in their boldness. They went on their merry business, making ready the feast, but there could never be a more unpleasant supper than the one they were about to have. For a goddess and a strong man were preparing their doom.

CHAPTER SEVENTEEN

Odysseus Bends the Great Bow

Athena now reminded Penelope of her plan. The faithful wife remembered the old bow as the subject of a contest which she was about to propose. She went up the lofty stairs and entered a distant room, where lay the treasures of Odysseus. She took down the bow from its peg. For a moment grief overcame her and she wept bitterly at the sight of the beloved bow. At last she brought the bow back with the arrows that were in the quiver. When she reached the hall she spoke aloud.

"Listen, proud suitors; you have stayed here on a perpetual celebration, eating and drinking my husband's wealth. Your excuse has been that you wish to marry me. Very well, then, take part in the contest I now propose. This is the great bow of Odysseus. I will promise to marry whoever is able to bend it most easily and send an arrow through the open part of twelve axes in a line. I will follow that man, leaving this house with all its wonderful memories."

As she finished, she ordered the swineherd to set the bow in place for the suitors. But Eumaeus was tearful as he took it. The herdsman Philoetius wept too when he saw his master's great bow. Seeing them weep, Antinous scolded them.

"You country fools, why do you weep and upset the poor lady? She is grief-stricken enough as it is over her husband's death. Either eat in silence, or leave the hall, leaving the bow up there. I think the contest will not be easy, for the bow will not be stretched too easily. I don't see a man here to compare with Odysseus, even though I remember him only from my own childhood."

As Antinous spoke, he hoped secretly that he'd be the one to bend the bow and send the arrow flying to its mark. He did not know that he'd be the first to taste the arrow from the hand of Odysseus, whom he had dishonored by his acts.

Telemachus addressed the suitors.

"I'm afraid I must be losing my wits. My mother is announcing that she'll go off with a husband and leave the house; here I am, laughing and happy over it. Well, come on, suitors, since the contest is on. There is no woman in Pylos, Argos, or Mycene like my mother. You know all that. I don't have to praise her. Come. No excuses. All of you will have your hand at trying to stretch this bow. I think I'll have a try at it myself. If I can stretch it and hit the target, I won't mind if my mother goes off and leaves me. Then I'll be able to protect my father's possessions."

As he finished, he thrust aside his purple cloak, took off his sword, and set up the axes, so that the openings in their heads were in a line. He went to the threshold and tried the bow. Three times he tried to

"I will promise to marry whoever is able to bend it most easily."

bend the great bow, but each time it resisted. He was about to force it the fourth time, but Odysseus signaled not to try again. Somewhat disappointed, Telemachus turned to the others and said, "Too bad. I'll turn out a weakling and a coward, or else in my youth I still do not have man's strength. At any rate, the rest of you come on for a try at the bow."

As he spoke he leaned the bow against the door and stood the arrow against the bow. Antinous cried out, "Rise in order to the right, all of you. Start from the place where the man is serving the wine."

The suitors were pleased at the arrangement. A man named Leiodes was first to try. He was a fairly decent sort who did not approve of the suitors' arrogance. He took the bow and tried it. He couldn't stretch it. His hands grew sore from the unsuccessful attempt. He turned to the rest and said, "Friends, I cannot stretch it. Let another try. This bow will be the death of many a chief, I fear."

Antinous was quick to scold him.

"Leiodes, what terrible thing are you saying? There's no reason to say the bow will be the death of many chieftains just because *you* can't stretch it. Your mother evidently didn't raise you to be a bow-stretcher. There are men here who will stretch it, don't you worry."

Suitor after suitor tried the bow. None could stretch it, even though Antinous and Eurymachus urged the suitors on. While the contest was going on, Odysseus went out, taking Philoetius and Eumaeus with him. When they were out of the hall, he said to them, "Herdsman and swineherd, I have some news. Shall I tell you or conceal it? My heart urges me to speak. If it came to fighting for Odysseus, how would you two men act? If he came out of nowhere, would you range yourself with him or with the suitors? Tell me the truth."

Philoetius spoke first.

"If Zeus would bring Odysseus back again, you'd see soon enough how I'd fight for him."

Eumaeus too prayed aloud that Odysseus might return soon. When Odysseus was assured of their loyalty, he said, "I am Odysseus, home again after twenty years. I know how you of all the servants truly welcome me. I haven't heard any of the others praying for my return! This is my plan for you. If Zeus helps me to slay the suitors, then I'll marry you both off and furnish houses and possessions for you. You'll be treated like comrades to Telemachus. I'll show you a sign to prove my words. Here is the scar which the boar inflicted on me during the boar hunt."

Having spoken, he drew back the rags from the great scar. When the two herdsmen were assured of his true identity, they wept aloud and embraced him, kissing his hands and shoulders. At last Odysseus restrained them.

"Enough, now. If anyone comes out and sees us, they'll tell the rest. Go in separately. I'll go first. This is the signal. All the suitors will refuse to let me try stretching the great bow. Then, Eumaeus, bring it to me. Tell the women to lock all the doors. Tell them to stay where they are, even if they hear noises and tumult inside. Philoetius, here is the key to the courtyard. Lock it at once."

Odysseus reentered the house, followed finally by the two faithful herdsmen. When he got back to the hall, Eurymachus was moving the bow about in his hands, warming it by the fire. Despite all this he couldn't stretch it, either. He groaned sadly and said, "Alas, I am very sorry for myself. I'm not concerned too much about the marriage. After all, there are many other beauties among the Greeks. What bothers me is this: if we are so much inferior to Odysseus in strength that we cannot stretch the bow, then our names will not be famous hereafter."

Antinous consoled him, saying, "Nonsense, Eurymachus. You know better than that. Today is a holy day. Who can stretch the bow on a day dedicated to the gods? Put it aside, but leave the axes where they are. No one will touch them. In the morning we'll renew the contest."

The suitors were happy at this compromise, but Odysseus spoke to them.

"Listen to me a moment, suitors, particularly Eurymachus and Antinous. Stop the contest now. In the morning Zeus will give strength to the right man. But come now. Let me try the bow. Let me see if I still have the strength I used to have, or if my troubles have weakened me."

The suitors were immediately indignant, fearing that perhaps he might stretch the bow. Antinous scolded him sharply.

"You wretched stranger, are you insane? You're not content to feast quietly among us. You're not content to listen to our conversation, though we allow no other beggar to do so. Now you want to try to stretch the bow! I warn you, if you do stretch it, we'll ship you off quickly to King Echetus, who loves to torture strangers. Drink quietly. Don't try to take part with younger men."

Penelope spoke up.

"Antinous, it's not decent or honorable to annoy the guests of Telemachus, whoever they may be. Do you expect the stranger to marry me if he does bend the bow? Such was never his intention. Don't worry about that."

Eurymachus replied, "No, Penelope, we don't expect him to carry you home. That isn't likely. But we do mind being held up to ridicule. People will say, 'Look here! These suitors must be weaklings. They can't bend the bow. Along comes a poor old beggar who does.' We can't allow such a situation to arise."

Penelope had an answer ready.

"Eurymachus, your good name is lost already for your actions here. You've already earned scorn because you have eaten the wealth of a great hero. This stranger looks sturdy. He claims to be of good family. Give him the bow. If he bends it, I'll reward him with a new tunic and cloak. I'll give him a sword and a javelin, too. And I'll provide him with new shoes. Let him try."

Telemachus broke in.

"Mother, I'm the one to decide who is to try the bow, no other. No one will force me to give the bow to the stranger, or to refuse it. Now you go back to your rooms, and watch over your own affairs. The bow is my concern. The power here is mine."

Penelope was astonished, but she went off obediently. Eumaeus took up the bow and carried it toward Odysseus. All the suitors scolded him unmercifully. At last someone spoke out aloud. "Where are you taking the bow, you villain of a swineherd? You'll soon be food for your own dogs if the gods approve."

Eumaeus was fearful for a moment and moved to return the bow. But Telemachus cried out, "Friend, bring the bow here. If you don't, I'll drive you out to the country with stones. I may be younger but I am stronger. I wish I were stronger than all these men; then I'd send them flying away from here."

The suitors thought this a good joke and laughed heartily, relaxing their anger for a moment. Eumaeus took advantage of the lull to give the great bow to Odysseus. Then he went out to Eurycleia and said, "Nurse, Telemachus would like you to lock all the doors. If anyone hears groaning, let him stay outside."

She went immediately to lock all the doors, while Eumaeus returned. Then Philoetius stole away and locked the courtyard gates. When he had finished, he went in and sat down, looking at Odysseus. Odysseus meanwhile was inspecting the bow, turning it around to make sure the worms had not injured it in his absence.

Someone nearby observed his actions and said to his neighbor, "This fellow must either be an admirer or a stealer of bows. Or perhaps he has one home like it. See how the old villain turns it in his hands."

His friend replied, "Little good he'll ever get out of stretching that bow!"

As they were speaking, Odysseus kept up his inspection. He bent the bow without difficulty. With his right hand he grasped the string and let it twang beautifully. During all this the suitors were amazed. Their color faded. Zeus sent forth a thunderclap as a favorable omen, and Odysseus was glad.

Odysseus picked up an arrow, which lay near him on the table. The others were stacked in the hollow quiver. Sitting where he was, he drew back the bow and let the arrow fly. Through the openings of all twelve axes flew the arrow. Odysseus turned to his son and said, "Telemachus, the stranger in the palace is not disgracing you. I haven't missed the mark. I have stretched the bow. My strength must be what it once was. These men must have been mistaken when they scorned me. But now it is time for your guests

He stood by his father, armed in shining bronze.

to prepare for their feast and to enjoy music and dancing."

As he spoke he gave the signal. Telemachus put on his sharp sword and grasped his spear. He stood by his father, armed in shining bronze.

CHAPTER EIGHTEEN

The Slaughter of the Suitors

Odysseus stripped aside the old rags he wore and leaped upon the threshold with his bow and arrow poised. He spread the arrows in front of him and cried out, "That contest has at last been won. Now I'll turn my attention to other targets."

With that he sent an arrow at Antinous. This carefree suitor was just about to lift a beautiful cup filled with wine. Death was far from his mind. After all, who among great numbers of feasters would expect that a single person would dare to attack! The shaft caught him in the throat, and the point pierced his neck. He sank back, and the cup fell from his lifeless hands. Blood spouted over the table, and he pushed aside the table with a jerk of his feet. All the food was spilled on the ground.

The suitors were in an uproar when they saw Antinous fall. They leaped from their seats and rushed off, looking for the armor that used to be on the walls. No shield or spear was anywhere to be seen. They cried out to Odysseus in their fury, "Madman, this is the last time you'll ever draw a bow. You have just slain the noblest man in Ithaca. The vultures will be dining off you very shortly."

Poor fools! They didn't realize that he had intended

to kill Antinous. They thought it was an accident. It didn't dawn on them how close to death they all were.

Odysseus cried out, "Dogs! You thought I'd never get back again from Troy. You thought you could continue to eat my food and insult my household. You thought you could woo my wife while I still lived. Your doom is sealed."

The suitors were terrified. They looked back and forth for a means of escape. Eurymachus alone had courage to speak.

"If you are indeed Odysseus, then you have spoken the truth about the evil doings in your house. But the man who was the cause of all this now lies dead— Antinous. It wasn't that he wanted a wife. He wanted to rule Ithaca after slaying your son Telemachus. Now he is slain instead. Please spare the rest of us. We will make it up to you."

Odysseus looked sternly at Eurymachus and said, "Even if you gave me everything you own, Eurymachus, you couldn't stop me from revenge. You have the choice of fighting or trying to escape—though I don't think many of you will escape."

The suitors were quaking with fright, but Eurymachus spoke up again.

"Friends, it's easy to see this man will not stop plans for slaughter. Since he has the bow and arrows, he'll continue to shoot until he has killed us all. Be men. Draw your swords and use the tables for shields. Let us all rush together against him, and try to thrust him from the threshold. Once we get outside we can raise an alarm. Then this man will shoot an arrow for the last time."

As he spoke he drew his sword and leaped at Odysseus with a piercing cry, but Odysseus sent an arrow at the same time that struck Eurymachus in the breast. Eurymachus threw his sword down and staggered around the table. He thrust all the cups and food on the ground as he lurched forth. He fell upon the ground and his forehead struck the dust. A shadow of darkness fell before his eyes, and he lay still.

Amphinomus rushed Odysseus next, his sharp sword flourished aloft. But Telemachus accounted for him, striking him from behind with his spear. It came out his chest and he fell with a thud. Telemachus rushed away, not even retrieving the spear, for he feared being struck if he tried to regain it. He ran to Odysseus and cried, "My father, now I'll bring you a shield, two spears, and a bronze helmet. I'll equip myself and the two faithful herdsmen. We must be armed."

Odysseus replied, "Run and get the arms while I still have arrows to defend myself with, or they may drive me from the threshold while I am alone."

Telemachus rushed out for reinforcements. He armed himself and the two servants, all three men taking their stand beside Odysseus. Meanwhile Odysseus sent forth the death-dealing arrows until the suitors piled up before him. When the arrows gave out, he stood the bow against a pillar and put on a shield and his famous helmet. He took also the two strong bronze-tipped spears which Telemachus had brought.

Now there was a certain door high up in the wall. This led to an alley outside. Odysseus warned the swineherd to guard this door, since there was only one approach. Agelaus had already thought of this and said to the others, "Friends, can't someone get through that door up there and raise the alarm? Then we can stop this slaughter."

But the goatherd Melanthius shook his head and said, "Not possible, Agelaus! One man can hold the fort there, for the doors are so narrow. Wait a minute. I'll bring you arms from the storeroom. I think I know where Odysseus and his son have stored the arms."

Then Melanthius went up through a secret way into the storeroom. He took out twelve shields and spears, and twelve helmets. He quickly carried them down and distributed them to the suitors.

When Odysseus saw this, he was dismayed, for the suitors were putting on the armor Melanthius had brought them. He turned to his son and said, "Telemachus, one of the women must be acting against us, or else it's Melanthius who's doing the job."

Telemachus replied, "Father, it's all my fault. I left the storeroom open, and their spy has found it. Eumaeus, close the storeroom door. Find out whether one of the women is the traitor, or Melanthius."

As they spoke Melanthius went in for another batch

of arms. This time Eumaeus spied him and said to
Odysseus, "The man we suspected is going for another
batch of arms. Shall I kill him myself, or bring him
here so that you can avenge yourself?"

Odysseus replied, "Telemachus and I will keep off
the attackers. You two go back and seize the traitor.
Bind him hand and feet and throw him into the storeroom. Hoist him up a bit on the rafters. Let him live
a while longer."

They went into the storeroom and surprised Melan-
thius, seizing him as he was leaving laden with arms.
They bound him and raised him off the ground. It was
Eumaeus's turn to scoff.

"Well now, Melanthius, you can be watchman to-
night. You'll see dawn at about the time you usually
bring in all the best goats for the suitors' feasts."

They left him there, struggling in his bonds. Putting on arms themselves, they went to the assistance
of Odysseus. Thus there were four of them ready to
face the survivors, among them many courageous men.

At this moment Athena appeared in the likeness of
Mentor, an old friend of Odysseus'. Odysseus was glad
to see her.

"Mentor," he cried, "help me in this fight. Remember me, an old friend who has often helped you."

As he said this, he guessed that this was really
Athena in human form. The suitors meanwhile spoke
threateningly. Agelaus said, "Mentor, don't let Odysseus persuade you to fight with him against us. If you

do, we'll kill you along with the others. And we'll take revenge on your wife and children, too."

Athena was furious at the words. She turned to Odysseus scornfully and said, "Odysseus, you're no longer the man you once were when you fought the Trojans. Then you killed many heroes. Troy was taken at last through your wisdom. What has happened? Now you have returned here and you *talk at* the suitors instead of *acting*. Come, my old friends; stand here and watch me to see how Mentor can repay old favors."

She ended, but did not bring about an overwhelming victory at once. She wished further to try the courage of Odysseus and Telemachus. In the shape of a swallow she fluttered off to the rafters and perched there.

Agelaus urged the suitors on to the battle. The most courageous of those still living circulated among the others, trying to boost their courage. Agelaus at last spoke to the group. "Friends, this man will weaken at last. See! Even Mentor has deserted him, and the four of them are left alone. Come. Don't all throw the spears at once. Six of us will throw first to try to wound Odysseus. The other men will be no concern if Odysseus is struck."

Six eagerly hurled their spears, but Athena turned them aside in their courses. They all struck uselessly elsewhere.

"Now, my friends," ordered Odysseus, "when I give

the signal, throw your spears into the mass of suitors. They would now add our deaths to the list of their abuses."

All four threw their spears together. Each one found a mark. Four of the suitors toppled over. The rest of the suitors rushed pellmell into the back of the hall. Odysseus and his men dashed to retrieve the four spears they had just sent forth. Once again the suitors sent their volley of spears, and once again Athena intervened. One spear grazed Telemachus' wrist and another slightly wounded Eumaeus. This was the extent of the damage.

Once more the four threw their deadly spears, and again four more suitors fell. The herdsman Philoetius accounted for Ctesippus. Standing over him, he boasted, "You foul braggart, this is your gift for the one you gave Odysseus when he came begging through the house."

Odysseus wounded another suitor in hand-to-hand combat, and Telemachus wounded a second. Then Athena caused the suitors to become panic-stricken. They rushed about aimlessly, like stampeding cattle. The four attackers pounced upon the suitors as vultures swoop down upon flocks of birds. The suitors fell on all sides, and the ground was soaked with blood. Leiodes rushed to Odysseus and fell on his knees before him, praying, "Pity me, Odysseus. I haven't done anything wrong. I tried to keep the other suitors from acting shamelessly, but they did not obey me. Their wickedness has brought on their fate. I have been only their prophet. I have done nothing; yet I am to die, too. There is no gratitude for good deeds."

But Odysseus was ruthless. "If you were their prophet, you must often have prayed that I'd not get back to my wife and home. You'll not escape death."

He took a sword which Agelaus had dropped when slain. He struck Leiodes on the neck and cut off his head.

But the harpist, who had entertained the suitors through no choice of his own, did escape death. The terrified man debated whether to rush from the room and pray before the altar of Zeus, or stay and pray to Odysseus. He decided to beg his life of Odysseus. Placing the harp on the ground, he fell on his knees before Odysseus.

"I pray that you'll honor me and pity me, Odysseus. If you kill me, a singer, your name will not be famous. God has inspired me with all kinds of songs, and I am able to sing to you as to a god. Do not kill me. Telemachus will vouch for me. He'll tell that I came here against my will."

Telemachus heard him and restrained his father, saying, "Don't kill this innocent man. We will save the herald Medon, too, for he always cared for me as a child—that is, if he's still alive."

Medon heard him. He lay crouching under a seat, covered with an oxhide for concealment. He rose at once and fell on his knees before Telemachus.

"O friend," he cried, "here I am. Don't let your father kill me in his rage at the suitors who have wasted his wealth."

Odysseus smiled and said, "Don't worry. My son has saved your life, so that you can be living proof that it's better to act honorably than evilly. Go on, now. Leave the hall and take the harpist with you. I still have some work to do."

The two rushed out, looking to right and left as they went, as if yet in fear of death. Odysseus combed the house to see if any of the men were still alive in concealment. The suitors were strewn out like fish in the nets of the fishermen, sprawling upon each other in death.

At last Odysseus addressed Telemachus.

"Son, call the nurse Eurycleia to me. I must tell her something."

Telemachus went to the door and called out, "Come here, old nurse. My father wants to speak to you."

Eurycleia hurried in, following Telemachus. She found Odysseus standing among the dead, spattered with blood. He looked like a lion that has devoured an ox. His breast and cheeks were covered with gore. When she saw the dead and all the blood, she began to raise a shout of praise, but Odysseus stopped her on the spot.

"Old woman," he said, "rejoice quietly. It is not holy to boast over the slain. The gods have brought these men low because they had no respect for anyone.

CHAPTER NINETEEN

Odysseus and Penelope

Eurycleia hurried upstairs as fast as her legs would carry her to break the good news to Penelope. She rushed in breathlessly and said, "Come, Penelope; come down and see what you have been hoping for these many years. Odysseus has returned! He has slain all the proud suitors, who destroyed his wealth and treated his son so insolently."

Penelope replied, "Poor nurse, the gods must have driven you insane. Why do you make fun of me in my sorrow by saying such nonsense? Why have you awakened me from my pleasant slumber? I've never slept so soundly since Odysseus went to Troy. You'd better go back downstairs. If any of the others had poked fun at me so cruelly, I'd have scolded her more severely. But I have pity on your age."

"I'm not making fun of you, my child," insisted Eurycleia. "Truly Odysseus has come back. He was the stranger in the palace, whom everybody scorned. Telemachus knew him for some time, but he concealed his knowledge until they could have revenge upon the suitors."

Penelope sprang happily from the bed and embraced the old woman.

"Tell me, nurse," said Penelope, "if Odysseus has

returned home as you say, how did he kill all the suitors? After all, he was but one against many."

"That I don't quite know," admitted Eurycleia; "but I did hear the groaning of the men as they were slain. The rest of us were terrified and hid in corners. Then Odysseus called for me. When I got there, I found Odysseus standing among the corpses. They were lying heaped upon one another. You would have been proud to see him like a lion among the slain.

"Now they're all packed together at the courtyard gate, and he is fumigating the house with sulphur. He sent me to get you. Come now, so that you both may be happy again. You've both had a hard time of it. Well, your prayers are answered at last. He has come back and found you and Telemachus in the palace. The suitors are all gone."

Penelope became cautious again and said, "Nurse, don't boast too much in your happiness. You know how welcome he'd be if he came. This tale can't be true, though. One of the gods must have slain the suitors for their evil deeds. They honored nobody, you know. Odysseus, I'm afraid, has lost his way far off and perished."

Eurycleia replied, "What *is* the matter with you, child? Did you think Odysseus would never come back? Your mind is always suspicious. I'll tell you another proof. I saw the very scar on his leg that a boar inflicted. I recognized it as I bathed him. I wished to tell you at once, but he refused to allow me then.

Come; come. I swear that I'm telling the truth. If I am lying, then kill me by the worst torture you can devise."

"Ah, nurse," answered Penelope, "it is difficult to know the ways of the gods. They are supreme tricksters. All right, I'll go down to my son, so that I may see the dead suitors and meet the man who slew them."

Saying this she went down the stairs. Her mind was confused. She debated whether to ask questions of her husband from a distance, or rush to him and embrace him. When she entered, she seated herself opposite Odysseus and sat a while in silence. He looked across at her, waiting for her to speak. She said nothing for a long time. At one moment she seemed to recognize him; at another he looked like a complete stranger, with his old rags for clothes.

At last Telemachus spoke impatiently.

"For heaven's sake, mother, why do you keep apart like that? You don't go near him! You don't question him! No other woman would hold herself aloof as you do after twenty years. Your heart must be harder than stone."

Penelope replied, "I am numb with shock. I cannot speak to him, or even look at him. If this is indeed Odysseus, then I'll know soon enough, for we have many secrets that only the two of us knew."

Odysseus smiled and said to Telemachus, "Let your mother try me; then she'll have no doubts. For the moment though, because I am in these rags, she cannot believe I am Odysseus. You and I have other worries. Consider this: if a man kills a single man with few relatives, he still flees his native land for fear of vengeance. But we have slain the finest youths of Ithaca! We must plan what to do next."

"Well, father," replied Telemachus, "you'd better do some thinking. Everybody has always told me that you were the brainiest person in the world, without a competitor. Whatever you say, the rest of us will do—no matter what."

Odysseus said, "This seems the best plan. Put on fresh clothing. Have the harpist strike up a merry tune so that neighbors will think there's a marriage being performed. No one must spread the rumor of the slaughter. Meanwhile we'll retreat to the farm and decide what to do next."

They did as he ordered and began the merry song. Outside a neighbor said, "Well, it looks as though the queen married at last. She couldn't guard the house for him until he came back. Heartless creature!"

After Odysseus had washed and dressed, Athena made him even more handsome and majestic to see. He returned to the hall and sat opposite Penelope.

"You're a strange person," he declared. "The gods have given you a heart of iron. No other woman would hold herself off from her husband after twenty years of suffering and separation."

"Sir," replied Penelope, "you are strange, too. I am not proud or indifferent. But I do have a very clear picture of you when you left Ithaca for Troy. Eurycleia, set the bed for him outside the room which he built himself. Put the bed outside, and make it up with rugs, blankets, and sheets."

This was Penelope's trap for her husband. He rose to the bait and said furiously, "Penelope, you're making me angry. Who has moved the bed? It would be very difficult for anyone to lift it, unless Zeus himself came to do the job. There is a secret in the construction of that bed. I made it myself, and no one helped.

"There was a sturdy olive tree growing in the courtyard. It was as thick, almost, as a pillar. I built the room around this tree. Then I cut off the leaves and smoothed the trunk. I polished it well and skilfully, and squared it true. The tree I made a bedpost. After this I constructed the rest of the bed. Thus you see I know the secret. I don't know whether the bed is still firm, or whether somebody has moved it, cutting off the foot of the olive tree."

She melted at these words, because she realized at last this was indeed Odysseus. Weeping, she ran forward and threw her arms around her husband, kissing him.

· "Don't be angry with me, Odysseus," she said; "you always were so understanding. The gods begrudged us the privilege of living our youth together. Don't be angry that I didn't rush at once into your arms when I saw you. I have always been terrified at the possibility that someone would trick me. But now, since you have told me the secret only the two of us knew, you have convinced me."

Odysseus was deeply moved. Finally he said, "Dear wife, we have not yet reached the end of our troubles. There are many problems ahead, as Tiresias foretold when I visited him in the land of the dead."

Penelope declared, "If the gods have planned a ripe old age for you, then there's hope that you'll get through all the problems that still lie ahead."

Then they began to talk of the long years between. Penelope told of the things she had to endure in the palace. Odysseus told of his adventures. He described the fight with the Ciconians, the land of the lotus-eaters, the horrible Cyclops. He bitterly told the story of Aeolus and the bag of winds. He related the slaughter by the Laestrygonians, and the adventures on the island of Circe. He described his visit to the land of the dead and the voice of the Sirens. He shuddered as he told about Scylla and Charybdis, and the slaughter of the cattle of the Sun. He mentioned his stay with Calypso, and emphasized his ever-expressed wish to return to Ithaca. At last he described the land of the Phaeacians and their treatment of him. By then it was nearly daybreak, but the two fell asleep for a little while.

In the morning Odysseus said to Penelope, "I must go to the farm to see my father, Laertes. He has been grieving for me. I think you'd better stay in your room all day, for a rumor about the slaughter of the suitors is bound to arise."

He put on his armor. Then he roused Telemachus and the two herdsmen, ordering them to put on their armor, too. They went out into the streets, but Athena shrouded them in a cloud, so that none could see them.

CHAPTER TWENTY

The Feud Is Ended

They soon reached Laertes' farm, which was snugly built and sturdy. Odysseus spoke to one of the servants outside. "Go indoors and kill the best pig you have. I am going to test my father to see if he recognizes me after all these years."

Odysseus gave his arms to the servants, and found his father alone in the vineyard. Laertes was carelessly dressed, for he worried constantly about his son and gave thought to little else. When Odysseus saw how miserable his father looked, he wept. He debated whether to rush up and embrace his father and tell him everything at once, or whether to question him first. He could not resist trying him first.

Odysseus went straight to Laertes and said, "Old man, you certainly do know how to manage an orchard! All the trees are certainly well kept. Don't be offended, though, if I say that you need some looking after yourself. Your master cannot be neglecting you, surely, because of your laziness. And you do look like a king in rags. Tell me; whose servant are you? Whose orchard are you taking care of? Tell me the truth: am I really in Ithaca as someone just told me? This fellow could not have been very intelligent, for I asked him about the ruler of this place. He gave me no information at all.

"Once, in my own country, I entertained a stranger who was most welcome. This foreigner boasted that he came from Ithaca, that his father was Laertes. I entertained him royally and gave him many gifts."

Laertes replied, "Stranger, you are indeed in Ithaca, but it is now held by the insolent suitors of my son's wife. You have wasted all the gifts you gave my son Odysseus. If he were here, he'd heap you with presents in return. But tell me, how many years is it since you entertained my son, that unfortunate guest of yours? Poor Odysseus! The fish have probably devoured him by now, or else the vultures have eaten his dead body on the shore. And nobody can give him proper burial and honor him in death. Tell me; who are you? Where do you come from? Where are your city and parents? Where is your ship beached, or did you come as a passenger on someone else's ship?"

Odysseus replied, "I'll tell you the absolute truth. My name is Eperitus. I come from distant Alybas, where I live in a mansion. I wandered here against my will from Sicania. My ship lies near a field far from the city. It was just five years ago that Odysseus left my country, but he did leave under good omens. He was happy when he left, for we heaped presents upon him."

At Odysseus' words the old man sank into despair.

He picked up the black dust and poured it over his white head and sobbed. Odysseus melted at the sight of his poor father. Rushing to him, he threw his arms about him and said, "I'm the one you've asked for, Dad. I'm back home after twenty long years. Stop sobbing. I have killed all the suitors and have had full revenge for their insolence and evil deeds."

Laertes looked up and said, "If you are indeed my son Odysseus, then give me a sign so that I can be sure."

Odysseus answered, "Look here; see the scar which the boar inflicted upon me. Yes, and let me describe the trees you gave me in this orchard. Remember how I used to follow you around the garden and beg for trees of my own? You gave me thirteen pear trees, ten apple trees, and forty fig trees. And you said you'd give me fifty rows of vines, with all kinds of grapes."

Laertes' knees trembled and his heart pounded faster, for he recognized the stranger as his son. He embraced him and said, "Father Zeus, the gods must still be in heaven if the suitors have paid for their insolence. But now I'm afraid that the families of the dead will be streaming out here to attack us."

Odysseus replied, "Don't worry, Dad. Now, let's go into the house. I sent Telemachus, the herdsman, and the swineherd on ahead to get supper."

They went in and found the other three preparing supper. Athena made Laertes stronger and taller, more majestic to the eye. When Odysseus saw him, he exclaimed, "Surely, Dad, some god has made you more noble to look at!"

Laertes replied, "I wish I were the man I once was when I captured Nericon, that strong fortress on the mainland. If I had been at your side yesterday, then I'd have accounted for many suitors. You'd have been proud of me."

Meanwhile, rumor of the death of the suitors spread rapidly through the city. The people gathered before the house of Odysseus with a great uproar. The families carried out their own dead and buried them. The dead from other cities they sent back by ship. They gathered in the market place, in desperate mood. When they had all come together, Eupithes got up to speak. He was the father of Antinous, the man Odysseus slew first of all.

"Countrymen," he said, "Odysseus has committed a fearful crime against all the Greeks. Many of us he took away and lost in those ships of ours. Others he slew on his return—many fine youths, too! Let's have some action before this man escapes. If he does, we'll never hold up our heads again. If I do not avenge my son's death, I prefer to be dead. Come; move quickly. Don't let them get away."

The people were moved to pity by his words and his tears. But Medon and the harpist whom Odysseus had spared pushed to the front. Medon shouted out,

"Listen a moment, men of Ithaca. Odysseus did these deeds with the consent of the gods. I myself saw one of the immortals standing next to him in the likeness of Mentor. This god helped Odysseus in the fight, and cast panic among the suitors."

The audience trembled at these words. An old hero took this opportunity to say, "Men of Ithaca, hear what I have to say. These deeds were brought on by your own wickedness. You refused to listen to me and to Mentor when we advised you to stop your sons from their actions. They acted evilly, wasting the property and insulting the wife of a great and excellent man, because they thought he'd never come back. Follow my advice. Don't go. Someone may suffer harm if he does."

Some applauded his words. Others still felt that the plan of Eupithes was best. These others rushed to put on their armor and marched out with Eupithes at the head. He vowed that he'd have revenge for his son's death. Little did he know that he would fall first.

In Olympus Athena spoke to her father, Zeus, saying, "O my father, let me ask you this. What are you planning now? Are you going to bring on war and strife? Or will you make peace between the two parties?"

Zeus, lord of the thunderbolt, replied, "My child, why do you ask me these things? Wasn't it your plan that Odysseus should return and have revenge upon the suitors? Do what you think best, but I'll tell you what I think is wise. Since Odysseus has had his revenge and has sworn faithful vows, let him be king. We'll help the people to forget the deaths of their sons and brothers. We'll let them love one another as before, in peace and prosperity."

Athena needed little urging. Down she rushed from the heights of Olympus.

Meanwhile Odysseus had been warned of the approaching attackers. Odysseus' party, together with the servants, armed themselves and went out to meet the assailants. Athena approached them in the likeness of Mentor. Odysseus saw her and was glad. He turned to his son and said, "Telemachus, when you are in the thick of battle where the best men are proved, you will know how not to disgrace the line of your fathers. Our family has been famous over the earth for valor and manliness."

Telemachus replied, "You'll see, father, that I'll not disgrace our family."

Laertes rejoiced at his words and said, "What a day this is! I'm completely happy, for my son and his son are rivals in courage!"

Athena, who was standing near him, breathed strength into him as she said, "Laertes, brandish your spear and send it flying!"

Sending forth a prayer, he hurled the long spear and struck Epithes through the helmet. The spear passed right through helmet and cheek. His arms clashed as he fell dead to the ground. Then Odysseus

and his son fell upon those who were among the first
of the attackers. They beat them thoroughly with
swords and spears. Indeed they would have slain the
entire company had not Athena cried out, "Stop your
fighting, men of Ithaca. Let the bloodshed cease."

At Athena's words the fighters trembled and dropped
their weapons. They turned and went back to the city,
anxious for their lives. Odysseus gave a mighty shout
and swooped upon them like a high-flying eagle. But
Zeus sent forth a mighty thunderbolt as a warning.
It fell before the feet of Athena. She turned to Odysseus and said, "Son of Laertes, noble Odysseus, stop
this warfare. Otherwise Zeus will be angry with you."

He obeyed her words gladly. Afterward, in the likeness of Mentor, Athena made both sides swear vows
of peace. Thus was the strife ended.

THE END

THE TROJAN WAR

Many references are made in the *Odyssey* to the famous Trojan War. Indeed, were it not for the Trojan War, the *Odyssey* could not have been written. For it was Odysseus' return from the war which inspired the story. How did this famous war start? The legendary explanation follows:

ORIGIN

Once at a wedding all the gods had been invited to attend except the Goddess of Discord. In her rage she hit upon a means of revenge. She threw an apple among the guests. Upon the apple was the inscription, *For the Fairest*. Naturally, the goddesses present were vainly concerned over the award of the apple. Three contestants claimed it: Hera, wife of Zeus; Athena, goddess of wisdom; and Aphrodite, goddess of love and beauty.

Not wishing to make a decision himself, Zeus sent the goddesses to Mount Ida, where Paris, Prince of Troy, was tending his flocks. Each goddess sought to win the decision. Hera promised Paris wealth and power. Athena pledged him fame in battle. But Aphrodite promised him the most beautiful woman for his wife. Forgetting his own beloved, Paris awarded the prize to Aphrodite.

With the help of Aphrodite, Paris sailed to Greece, where he was received graciously by Menelaus. The bride of Menelaus was Helen, whose beauty had attracted many suitors before her marriage to Menelaus. Again with Aphrodite's help Paris carried off Helen to Troy. Menelaus immediately called upon all the other Greeks for help. They had all agreed to support whomever Helen had chosen as husband.

The Greeks came forward to his assistance. Some were reluctant to come. Odysseus, for example, loved his wife Penelope and son Telemachus so dearly that he pretended madness, so the others would leave him behind. But the chiefs who came for him were cunning, too. As he was plowing, they placed his infant son in front of the plow. Odysseus turned it aside, thus revealing his sanity.

Even the greatest hero of all, Achilles, did not come forth readily. His mother, Thetis, a goddess herself, realized the fate in store for Achilles if he went to war. She tried to hide him among the women, dressed as a young girl. But Odysseus, now won over to the cause, found him out by going among the women in the guise of a merchant. He mixed arms with the female jewelry he was selling. When Achilles handled the armor and not the jewels, Odysseus knew him at once and persuaded him to join the expedition.

Agamemnon was chosen leader of the Greeks. Other Greek heroes includedAjax, Diomed, and Nestor. The Trojans had many famous warriors on their side, too. Foremost was Hector, generous and noble. Others were Aeneas, Deiphobus, and Sarpedon. Aeneas, ac-

cording to legend, was to be the founder of **Rome.**
For the story has it that after the Trojan War, he left
and landed eventually in Italy, where he became **a**
leader. The Roman writer Virgil's epic tale, **the**
Aeneid, is the story of his adventures.

AT TROY

After many adventures the heroes landed at Troy
and fought bitterly for nine long years without victory. There was a legend that Troy would not be taken
before two famous Greek leaders disagreed. The disagreement came in the tenth year. This disagreement
is the subject of Homer's *Iliad,* the companion epic to
the *Odyssey.*

During the nine years the Greeks had plundered
many of the Trojan allies, though they had been un-
able to touch Troy itself. On one of their expeditions
they had taken many captives, among them a maiden
named Chryseis. She fell to Agamemnon as part of
the spoils. But her father, a priest of Apollo, prayed
for vengeance. The god Apollo heard his prayer and
sent a pestilence upon the Greeks.

In the midst of the plague Achilles accused Agamemnon of being the cause of their bad luck by his
refusal to yield Chryseis. Agamemnon agreed at last
to yield the girl, but he angrily demanded instead one
of Achilles' captives. Achilles submitted to his com-
mander-in-chief, but declared his part in the war **was**
over. He withdrew to his tents in a rage.

Fortune began to turn against the Greeks. Without Achilles the attackers found themselves handicapped. In a bitter two-day battle the gods and goddesses took sides, some with the Greeks, others with the Trojans. The Trojan Hector performed many feats of valor, as the fight grew more bitter.

Events turned from bad to worse for the Greeks. In desperation Patroclus, Achilles' closest friend, appealed to Achilles. The great hero relented a bit, allowing Patroclus to wear his armor and lead his men into battle. In the thick of the fight Patroclus met Hector and was slain. Hector took the armor as spoils of war.

The death of Achilles' friend accomplished what all the pleadings of the Greeks had not done. Achilles agreed to return to the conflict, arrayed in a new suit of armor. His revenge was terrible, for he singled out Hector and slew him. To add shame, he dragged the body of Hector before the eyes of the Trojans. At last Priam, the old King of Troy, father of Hector, went to beg Hector's body for decent burial. Moved by the sight of the old man, Achilles granted his request.

So ends the *Iliad*. But other legends complete the story of the Trojan War.

Achilles in turn was slain by Paris, who was himself killed soon after. Odysseus and Ajax contested possession of the famous armor of Achilles. When the prize was awarded to Odysseus, Ajax killed himself.

The *Odyssey* tells of Odysseus' meeting with Ajax's unforgiving spirit (page 74).

THE WOODEN HORSE

Troy was finally taken by a trick, not by force. Odysseus advised the Greeks to build a huge, hollow wooden horse. Inside he put a group of fighting men, armed to the teeth. The rest of the Greeks pretended to sail away. The Trojans rushed from the city, jubilant at the disappearance of the Greeks. One priest, Laocoon, urged the destruction of the horse. He cast his spear at the horse, and it sent forth a hollow sound. The Trojans might have followed his advice, but just then a captive was brought in. The captive was a Greek, who had been left behind through the malice of Odysseus—*he said!* He declared that the horse was an offering to Athena, that it had been made too big to be carried inside the city. If the Trojans were able to get it inside, he said, then they'd surely triumph over the Greeks.

The Trojans wavered. To make their deception complete, two huge sea serpents, sent by a god, slithered over the sands and devoured Laocoon with his sons. The Trojans hesitated no longer, thinking Laocoon's fate an omen. They managed to get the horse into the city, and spent the evening in celebration. In the middle of the night the Greeks poured forth from the Horse and opened the city's gates. The rest of the

Greek army poured into the city. Troy was completely destroyed.

THE HOMECOMINGS

A few of the Trojans were made captive. The rest were slain. Then the Greeks prepared to go home after ten years. Menelaus returned with Helen. We meet the two, apparently completely happy, on page 115 of the *Odyssey*. Agamemnon took the captive Trojan maiden Cassandra with him, and set out. His fate is described by his spirit on page 71. Odysseus left with his ten ships, but was destined to reach home without a ship, without a comrade. The story of his adventures is the magnificent story of the *Odyssey*.

THE BACKGROUND OF THE ODYSSEY

ODYSSEUS IN OTHER STORIES

How is Odysseus presented in other literary works? Is his character consistent throughout? Not entirely!

The Odysseus of the *Iliad* is not too different from the Odysseus of the *Odyssey*. He is pictured as a wise leader, a prudent fighter, a man able to bring together warring groups. He is considered wily and clever, but there is a nobility about him that commands respect. He is chosen to help settle differences between people and is one of those who urge Achilles (page 226) to return to the battle. He is recognized by everyone as a great leader and is often mentioned along with Agamemnon, the leader of the Greek army. He is last mentioned in the *Iliad* after a victory over Ajax in a sporting contest. In the *Odyssey* there is a sequel to this event. Even after death, Ajax will not forgive him, as we learn during Odysseus' visit to the Land of the Dead (page 74).

In the *Aeneid,* which is written not from the point of view of the Greeks but from the point of view of the Trojan hero Aeneas, Odysseus (here called "Ulysses") is portrayed much less favorably. He is called "ruthless" and "terrible." As he leaves the Wooden Horse (page 227) he leads the final attack on defenseless Troy. Aeneas looks upon Odysseus as a cruel, tricky, evil man. But we must remember that this is a description given by his enemies.

In Canto XXVI of the 13th century Italian poet Dante's *Inferno,* Odysseus is again portrayed by "the other side." (The Italians traced their ancestry to Rome and Aeneas.) Sunk in the Eighth Circle of Hell, Odysseus suffers the fate of the Evil Counselors, men who have used their great skill for fraud and deception. When questioned, Odysseus tells of how he sailed beyond the Pillars of Hercules below the Equator to die in a shipwreck near the Mount of Purgatory.

Odysseus appears as a character in many other works, including a play by Shakespeare, *Troilus and Cressida,* but nowhere do we get to know him as we do in the *Odyssey,* where he is portrayed sympathetically and fully. He is a man of many qualities. Some of his weaknesses are seen there, too, but on the whole he is a man of good character and ability.

WHAT IS AN EPIC?

The *Iliad* and the *Odyssey* are considered two of the world's greatest epic poems. What is meant by an epic? As usually understood, an epic is a long poem that tells a story about great heroes. Usually one hero is the central figure. He is larger than life, a man of great skill, wisdom, cunning, and strength. Achilles, the central figure of the *Iliad,* is a great warrier, the greatest of his time. Odysseus, the hero of the *Odyssey,* possesses great cunning and strength. After enduring hardships that would destroy an ordinary man, he emerges triumphant.

Usually epics are associated with particular nations or peoples. They show the ideals and hopes of these people. The Sumerian *Gilgamesh,* the Spanish *El Cid,* the Finnish *Kalevala,* the Anglo-Saxon *Beowulf,* the Indian *Mahabharata,* and the German *Nibelungenlied* all contain legends familiar to the people of the nation that produced them.

Some epics can be traced to particular authors. The *Iliad* and the *Odyssey* are usually considered to have been written by Homer, but some scholars doubt the existence of one man called Homer (page 242). The *Aeneid,* discussed below, is the work of the Roman poet Vergil, who wrote in Latin. The Italian poet Dante composed the *Divine Comedy.* The English poet John Milton wrote *Paradise Lost.* The *Aeneid,* the *Divine Comedy,* and *Paradise Lost* are sometimes called "literary epics," in contrast with the folk epics mentioned in the preceding paragraph.

GILGAMESH

The earliest epic of which we have any record is the Sumerian tale of Gilgamesh, the heroic king of Erech, who sets out on a quest that in some ways resembles the *Odyssey.* Gilgamesh may have been an actual king in the land of Sumer (today, part of Iraq) 5000 years ago. As often happens, the legend surrounding him has come down to us, but the actual facts of his reign have disappeared—if indeed he ever existed.

According to the tale, Gilgamesh has offended the

gods by his actions. To punish him, the gods send to earth an opponent, Enkidu, to challenge him. Enkidu, who has been made from mud and brought to life, is a powerful warrior whose strength seems irresistible. Enkidu is lured by a trick into the city, where Gilgamesh, after a fierce struggle, defeats him and then accepts him as a friend.

After a dream, Gilgamesh resolves to do battle with a fire-breathing monster who guards the cedar forests. Though he is urged by Enkidu and others not to persist, he decides to follow his impulse. Enkidu, unwilling to desert his friend, goes along. Gilgamesh kills the monster, but the goddess Ishtar sends a mighty bull against the bold hero. As Gilgamesh is losing this battle, Enkidu rushes in and saves his friend by killing the bull.

Unfortunately for the two heroes, the bull is sacred. The gods rule that Enkidu must die for his actions. Stricken with an illness, Enkidu lingers for twelve days and dies on the thirteenth day.

Though Gilgamesh is himself part god, he suddenly realizes that he too may be mortal. Fearing death, because he has seen his friend die, Gilgamesh travels over the earth to find immortality. His wanderings are fantastic and wonderful, like those of Odysseus. At last he comes to the home of Utnapishtim, who has been granted eternal life by the gods. Utnapishtim reminds Gilgamesh of every man's mortality, but he does provide an apparent way out. He tells of a plant that grows at the bottom of the sea, a plant that gives eternal life. After many more adventures, Gilgamesh gets the plant. On the way home, however, the plant is stolen by a snake, and Gilgamesh is left with the realization that he too must die.

There are many similarities between *Gilgamesh* and the Homeric epics. The gods participate in the affairs of men, and in their anger they sometimes seem less than superhuman. Gilgamesh sees marvels and monsters at every turn. There is even an episode in which Gilgamesh talks with the ghost of his friend Enkidu. What Enkidu has to say about life after death resembles what Achilles says (page 73) in the *Odyssey*. The friendship of Gilgamesh and Enkidu resembles that of Achilles and Patroclus in the *Iliad*.

Gilgamesh is a remarkable epic by any standards, but it is even more wonderful if we consider its date. It came more than 1500 years before the Homeric epics. In his introduction to *Gilgamesh,* N. K. Sandars says Gilgamesh is ". . . the first tragic hero of whom anything is known. He is at once the most sympathetic to us, and most typical of individual man in his search for life and understanding, and of his search the conclusion must be tragic."

BEOWULF

Does England have a great national epic, too? The answer is *yes*—with an explanation. There is a famous epic written in Old English, but the events described have no relationship to the land of England itself! The explanation for this strange situation lies in the history of the English language and the English people.

Very little is known about the earliest inhabitants of England, but we do know something about the people who followed them, the Celts. It was the Celts who were present when the Roman legions conquered England nearly two thousand years ago. It was the Celts who remained when the Roman legions abandoned the island about A.D. 410. Soon after the Romans left, the Angles and the Saxons, invading tribes from northern Europe, conquered the Celts. These newcomers established their language, Anglo-Saxon, as the language of England. Though the English language has had many influences and many additions, Anglo-Saxon remains its basic ingredient language. Anglo-Saxon gave English its structure and a great many of its most frequently used words.

When the Angles and Saxons came from the continent, they brought with them the legends and stories they liked to tell in their original homeland. One of the legends was the tale of Beowulf, a hero of southern Sweden. The epic is set in Denmark and Sweden, not in England. But the Anglo-Saxons first wrote the story down soon after A.D. 1000 and added some ingredients of their own. Thus, the epic is associated with the English language.

Epics often have some historical basis. There may have been a hero named Beowulf and some of the story elements may be based on fact. There are allusions to a raid that took place in the sixth century. The story as we now have it, however, is almost completely legendary.

The epic tale of *Beowulf* can be divided into two part: a section dealing with the exploits of Beowulf's young manhood and a section dealing with the heroism of his old age.

The beginning of the story sets a mood of terror. For twelve years a monster, Grendel, has been roaming the countryside of Hrothgar, King of the Danes. His evil has been unchecked, and he has killed many of the king's stalwart warriors. He frequently stalks into the hall of the king, seizing warriors as they sleep and eating them on the spot. As he leaves, he grasps others to take back with him to his den beneath the waters of his marshland home.

Across the sea, in southern Sweden, mighty Beowulf hears of the monster's ravages and resolves to aid the unlucky kingdom of Hrothgar, for Beowulf's father has been a close friend of Hrothgar's. He leaves his native land of the Geats and sails for Denmark with a faithful band of fourteen men. When they arrive in Denmark, they are welcomed and feasted in the great banquet hall. After the feasting, as is their custom, the warriors of Hrothgar lie down to sleep. Beowulf, with his little band, stands guard.

As usual, Grendel comes in and seizes a sleeping warrior, but this time he is met by a force greater than any

he has ever encountered before. Beowulf, without paus-
ing to seize shield or spear, grips Grendel and with his
incredible strength wrenches the arm off the terrible
monster. Thus badly wounded, Grendel flees to his
home in the marshes, and his arm is hung in the hall as
a trophy.

There is no end of the terror, however, for the next
night Grendel's mother comes to seek revenge. She
seizes an important counselor of the king, takes the arm
of Grendel, and with both prizes flees to her home
beneath the waters. This time she is unchallenged, for
Beowulf is sleeping in another house and doesn't learn
of the new attack till morning.

A band sets out, with Beowulf at the head. They
come to the marsh and discover the head of the counselor, but they see no sign of Grendel's mother. Beowulf
realizes that he will have to meet the monster on her
own ground and on her own terms. Without hesitating,
he slips beneath the waters and seeks the cave in which
she lives.

After fighting off other dangers, Beowulf arrives at
the monster's den. Then follows a bitter hand-to-hand
struggle in which Beowulf is gradually being defeated.
Fortunately, he spies a magic sword lying in the cave.
He quickly picks it up and slays the monster. He cuts
off the head of the wounded Grendel and swims back to
the surface.

There is great rejoicing and feasting at the happy
outcome of this struggle, and peace settles on the land

of Hrothgar. But the time must come for Beowulf's return to his own homeland, and he takes leave of his new friends.

After a time Beowulf becomes king of the Geats and rules successfully for fifty years. There is, however, one final battle for Beowulf to wage.

One day one of Beowulf's subjects discovers a treasure hoard and steals it while the dragon who guards it is sleeping. When the dragon awakes, he goes on a rampage, devastating the land. Though an old man, Beowulf resolves to face the dragon.

Beowulf comes upon the dragon and engages him in combat. The battle is long and hard, and Beowulf begins to lose. Once again he is forced to use his mighty hands, but still the struggle goes against him. Then Wiglaf, the only warrior who has stayed behind to help, strikes the dragon with his sword. Beowulf is thus able to use his war-knife and give the dragon a mortal wound, but not before Beowulf himself is fatally hurt. His countrymen mourn his death, for he was the protector of his people. They are left at the end fearing an invasion by their enemies.

From *Gilgamesh* to *Beowulf* is a jump of several thousand years, but there are similarities between the two tales. In both epics a mighty hero overcomes great odds in the eternal struggle with the forces of evil. Both have to overcome powerful monsters. Both have to sink beneath the sea during their quests. Both are aided by trusted friends in the struggle with their nonhuman opponents. Both epics end tragically.

There are of course similarities between *Beowulf* and the *Odyssey* too. The man-eating habits of Grendel are similar in many ways to the cannibalism of Polyphemus (page 41) and the Laestrygonians (page 53). The way in which Grendel seizes the warriors reminds a reader of Scylla (page 84). The superhuman power of Beowulf reminds us of Odysseus at his best—in the land of the Phaeacians (page 27) and in Ithaca (page 194).

The durability and great age of the epic *Gilgamesh* are more striking when we realize that we are much closer in time to *Beowulf* than Homer to *Gilgamesh!* For another look at the time scale of the events we are describing see also pages 243-246.

THE AENEID

Of all the other epics, the *Aeneid* is of most interest to readers of Homer because it deals with some of the same events that Homer speaks of. Aeneas, son of King Priam of Troy, is driven by a storm to Carthage on the northern coast of Africa. At Carthage, in the presence of Queen Dido, he tells the story of his wanderings, much as Odysseus tells his story to King Alcinous of the Phaeacians (pages 33-34).

Aeneas relates the story of the fall of Troy. He tells about the Trojan Horse (page 227). He describes the slaughter of the luckless Trojans by the treacherous and cruel Greeks. He explains his own escape and talks about the dangers he has experienced in his wanderings.

Aeneas must wander further, however, and he leaves Carthage with his company. After a time he arrives in Italy. Like Odysseus, he goes down to the underworld to speak to the dead. The shade of his father tells Aeneas that he will be the founder of a great nation that will be called "Rome."

Aeneas has many adventures before he finally overthrows his rival, Turnus. He wins the hand of the beautiful Lavinia and then fulfills his destiny, becoming the founder of Rome.

The *Aeneid,* like the *Odyssey,* is a sequel to the *Iliad.* It is told from the Trojan point of view and provides a different picture of some of the Greek heroes. (See also page 229.) Unlike the *Iliad* and the *Odyssey,* the *Aeneid* is clearly and certainly the work of one man. We know when it was created and for what purpose: to glorify Rome. Though not so famous or so widely read as the Homeric tales, the *Aeneid* has maintained a steady popularity through the centuries.

THE ARGONAUTS

Even today the sea is a terrible opponent. Every year there are many disasters at sea, even though man has been gathering knowledge about the sea for thousands of years. Sudden storms, human error, faulty construction of ships—all these play a role in accidents at sea.

The Greeks, being a seafaring people, were fully

aware of the dangers all sailors faced. Homer is filled with references to the sea in all its many moods. Greek seamen had a healthy respect for the waters they had to sail upon. They appreciated good sea stories like the *Odyssey*. In addition to the *Odyssey* there are other seafaring tales in Greek mythology. The story of the voyage of the good ship *Argo* is one of the most famous.

The *Argo* is associated with Jason, who sets out on a strange quest. Jason's task is to steal the Golden Fleece, the priceless skin of a mythical ram. The fleece, hanging on a tree by the shore of the Black Sea, is guarded by a dragon that never sleeps.

To help him on his quest, Jason gathers together one of the greatest companies any hero ever led: Hercules, Orpheus, Castor and Pollux, and Theseus, among others. These Argonauts, as they are called, face obstacles and adventures that resemble those of Odysseus.

Jason is successful in his quest. He has had the assistance of the witch Medea, whom he later marries. The later tragedy of Jason's faithlessness and Medea's murder of their two children in vengeance is told in *Medea,* the great play by Euripides. But it is the earlier tales, involving the sea, that remind us most of the *Odyssey*.

THE SHIPS OF ODYSSEUS

At Mystic Seaport, in Connecticut, a restored seaport of the nineteenth century, visitors are allowed to explore the only wooden whaling ship that has survived from the great whaling fleets of a hundred years ago. The ship, the *Charles W. Morgan,* is over a hundred feet long and spacious by the standards of its day. To our eyes, however, the quarters seem cramped for the thirty-seven men who shipped aboard her for years at a time. Below the main deck the men had to stoop as they made their way from their quarters to the gangways. The bunks themselves are huddled together, with every inch of space accounted for. Eating facilities are makeshift: barrels for tables and chairs. Down in the hold the kegs of whale oil were tightly packed.

As the visitor pauses, looks around, and imagines what life was like then, he gets, at least for a moment, the feeling of being at sea with only the ship beneath his feet for survival.

If you ever have an opportunity to go aboard a historic vessel, or its replica, take advantage of the opportunity. Whether it is the tiny vessels at Jamestown, Virginia, or the *Constellation* at Baltimore, you will enjoy the experience and you will better understand the *Odyssey.* For the *Odyssey* is a sea story told in infinite detail and with sparkling vitality. To feel as Odysseus and his men felt, however, you must put yourself imaginatively in his place.

What was his boat like? Unlike the seagoing *Charles W. Morgan* mentioned above, the ships of Odysseus' time were not meant for long voyages across the open sea. They were built for short trips within sight of the shore, with the ship putting in at night at a safe harbor.

They carried both sails and oars, for the winds on the Mediterranean are sometimes undependable. The ships had movable masts. The sails were used only in moderate winds and were made of either papyrus or linen.

An interesting characteristic of ships of the period is the "oculus" or eye painted on both bows. The custom, still surviving today, goes back to ancient Egypt, when Egyptian seamen painted the eye of Ra, the Sun God, on their vessels.

Because the winds were undependable, the vessels of Odysseus relied heavily upon oarsmen. Since oarsmen had to work in shifts, each ship had to carry a large number of men. Ernle Bradford estimates that Odysseus had about five hundred men in his twelve ships. If this were so, each ship carried about forty men.

Although mythology has recorded the name of the *Argo,* the famous vessel of the Argonauts, we do not know the name of Odysseus' ships. Still we become familiar with these ships, for the *Odyssey* has many references to them.

WAS THERE A HOMER?

> Seven cities warred for Homer being dead,
> Who living had no roof to shrowd his head.
> Thomas Heywood

About this most famous of epic poets we know very little indeed. A dozen cities claimed him, but no one knows for sure where he was born. In ancient times biographies of Homer were circulated, but these were pure fiction.

Some authorities assert he never existed. Others say there were two Homers: the author of the *Iliad* and the author of the *Odyssey*. Samuel Butler had the most original theory: he said that Homer was really a woman who put herself into the narrative as Nausicaa!

Homer is usually represented as blind, perhaps because there are references to two blind bards in the *Odyssey*. (See page 25, where Demodocus is introduced.)

We have a more recent parallel to this confusing situation. Today there are those who insist that Bacon, or someone else, wrote the plays of Shakespeare. Guesses are entertaining but do not necessarily add to our knowledge. As far as Homer is concerned, most authorities are content to talk about him as a real person who lived about 800-700 B.C.

There were at least eight ancient Greek epics, but only the *Iliad* and the *Odyssey* have survived in complete form. Of the great Greek plays, written much later than Homer, only a fraction have survived. Of the other great works of ancient times, we have only a tiny sample. But we do have the *Iliad* and the *Odyssey*, a tribute to the respect accorded these two great poems from the past.

PLACING THE ODYSSEY IN TIME

Some people conveniently divide history into three

ages: the ancient, the medieval, and the modern. The only difficulty with this simplified division is the lack of perspective with regard to the ancient world. It lumps together the time of the Great Pyramids and the time of Augustus, the first Roman emperor. But Augustus is closer to us in time than he is to the Pharaohs who built those pyramids. When Augustus ruled his empire (27 B.C.-A.D. 14), the Great Pyramids were already nearly 3000 years in the past.

If we set the Great Pyramids at one point in our time scale (about 2900 B.C.) and Augustus at the other end, where do Homer and the *Odyssey* fit in? They belong somewhere in between, but again closer to Augustus than to the builders of the Old Kingdom in Egypt!

First of all, we must realize that Homer is *not* telling about events in his own time. Some authorities date Homer about 800 B.C. (See also pages 253-257.) The events told in the *Iliad* and the *Odyssey* are about four centuries earlier, soon after 1200 B.C. Thus there is as long a gap between Homer and the events he tells about as there is between our time and the Spanish Conquests of Mexico and Peru. If we realize how many gaps there are in our knowledge of this period, we can appreciate the difficulties of transmitting a whole epic through so many centuries without writing it down.

There are many clues to tell us that the poems were composed at a much later date than the events they describe. One of the most interesting is Homer's quoting a proverb about iron. This is a reference to Homer's own time. The heroes of the *Odyssey* are heroes of the Bronze Age, before the widespread use of iron for weapons.

By the sixth century B.C., scholars had already begun to study the *Odyssey* and the *Iliad*. Thus for more than 2500 years both books have been under critical examination and have been read for pleasure also. The Athenian statesman Pisistratus, who lived in the sixth century B.C., is said to be the first who had the text of Homer's works written down.

The *Odyssey* and the *Iliad* have been translated into all the important languages of the world. According to L. Sprague de Camp and Catherine C. de Camp in *Ancient Ruins and Archaeology,* "The translations alone would fill the bookshelves of a room, and the commentary would require a whole library." No literate person in the western world should be unfamiliar with these books.

Are the events described by Homer historical? At one time men thought not. They assumed that the books were mythical, pure stories to entertain, stories without foundation in fact. But after Heinrich Schliemann began to uncover the site of Homer's Troy, in 1871, scholars began to think differently. Then Sir Arthur Evans uncovered the palaces of Minos at Knossos in Crete in 1899. Only a few years ago the palace of Nestor (page 74) was uncovered. This find showed the truth behind another portion of the Homeric legends.

Every passing year, as excavations continue around

the world, we learn more about the past. Books written only fifty years ago about ancient civilizations are incomplete and out of date. Each new discovery opens new doors.

The publication of C. W. Ceram's *Gods, Graves and Scholars* some years ago sparked a tremendous interest in archaeology. Dozens of popular books on the subject have since appeared. The magazine *Archaeology* appeals to a great many laymen. Television programs have told the story of archaeology and have popularized the romance of sites like that at Stonehenge in England.

We are more curious about our past, for we find in our past many lessons for the present. For our understanding of people and customs of the past we owe a great deal to the *Iliad* and the *Odyssey*.

HEINRICH SCHLIEMANN

Sometimes truth is indeed stranger than fiction. One of the greatest archaeologists of the last century, Heinrich Schliemann, spent a good part of his adult life as a businessman, not a scholar. Yet he succeeded where scholars failed and proved the truth of some of his own theories, despite the opposition of many men supposedly more learned than he.

Heinrich Schliemann was born in 1822 into a poor German family. As a child, he lived in the village of Ankershagen, where old ruins stimulated his always vivid imagination. Often, his father told the impressionable child tales of Pompeii and the Trojan War. One Christmas the boy received a book containing an artist's imaginative print showing the ancient Scaean Gate to Troy. Everything worked together to arouse Heinrich's interest in the past, particularly the time of ancient Troy.

For a time the demands of life turned Schliemann's attention to other fields, however, and he became a very successful businessman. Schliemann was so successful that he was able to retire from business while still a young man. He immediately devoted his attention to his real interest, the study of the past.

About a hundred years ago, when Schliemann began his search for Troy, archaeology was hemmed in by ignorance and prejudice. Some scholars, for example, argued that Troy had never existed and that the tales of Homer had no basis in fact. Schliemann, of course, disagreed. He never questioned the reality of Troy, and he set out to prove his statements. But where was he to look?

Ancient Greek tradition suggested that the Homeric city of Troy lay under the mound of Hissarlik in Asia Minor. Many later geographers disputed this site, however, even when they believed in the existence of a historical Troy. Since excavating is an expensive and wearying task, no one was interested in trying to find the answer—no one before Schliemann.

Using the resources of his private fortune, Schliemann began the excavation of Hissarlik. He hired over a hundred workmen and devoted more than eleven months, over a period of years, to these first diggings. He faced difficulties and obstructions that would have discouraged a less determined man. He had to guard against theft and official interference. As we have already noted above, however, his efforts met with success.

Schliemann spent a good portion of the rest of his life digging in Troy, though he also excavated many other areas of interest to archaeology. Many of his interpretations were challenged and his conclusions disputed, but he kept going. For twenty years he persisted in his efforts to uncover the past and to prove that there was a Scaean Gate, an Agamemnon, a Mycenae.

The many-layered city of Troy is today an archaeologist's paradise. Though not all details can be settled with certainty, most scholars now recognize the enormous contribution that Schliemann made in proving the existence of the places mentioned by Homer.

Perhaps you'd like to see what Heinrich Schliemann looked like. In C. W. Ceram's *The March of Archaeology,* you'll find many pictures of Schliemann as well as of the diggings at Troy and elsewhere. For a fascinating story of Schliemann's life, read Robert Payne's *The Gold of Troy.*

WERE THE WANDERINGS REAL?

What can we say about those marvelous wanderings

of Odysseus? How real are they? Certainly some of the places mentioned are real enough: Tenedos, the land of the Ciconians, Ithaca. But many questions remain. (Some scholars have even debated whether present-day Ithaca is the Ithaca of Odysseus.) Where is the Land of the Lotus Eaters? Where is Calypso's magic island, Ogygia? Does it really exist or is it pure fancy? And the Land of the Dead? Surely this exists only in never-never land.

Many scholars have puzzled over this problem. The ancient Greeks and Romans had their theories. Some theories have been passed down from generation to generation. Present-day tourists are told by natives with conviction that "this is where Odysseus was held prisoner by Polyphemus" or "here are the rocks of the Sirens." Some of these legends merely help bring tourist business, but others may have a basis in fact.

Thucydides, a Greek historian of 2500 years ago, identified many of Odysseus' ports of call with actual places in the Mediterranean. Five hundred years later another Greek, the geographer Strabo, sailed around the Roman world and wrote a geography, frequently quoting the *Odyssey*. In the last century the English novelist Samuel Butler was intrigued by the problem and suggested many solutions.

Perhaps the two most famous and most recent students of the route are Victor Berard and Ernle Bradford. Ernle Bradford, in his *Ulysses Found,* presents a fascinating and believable identification of lands mentioned in the *Odyssey*. His book was made the subject of a television program actually picturing the sites he identified. He and Berard agree with each other and with ancient writers on many details, but they differ in others. Since there is no universal agreement, each person must examine the evidence and decide for himself.

There is little difficulty with the early episodes in the wanderings. Tenedos, the land of the Ciconians, and the strait of Malea are all quite definite. The Land of the Lotus Eaters introduces some disagreements, though nearly all writers place this land in northern Africa. Bradford and others suggest that it is the island of Jerba (or Djerba) off the coast of Africa.

The Land of the Cyclopes and the island of Polyphemus produce differences of opinion, too. Bradford names Trapani, Sicily, as the area described by Homer, but Berard prefers the Gulf of Naples. The Island of Aeolus produces broad areas of disagreement. Bradford says it is an island north of Sicily called Ustica. The ancients identified it in the Lipari group, and others chose Stromboli. (Bradford chooses Stromboli, too, but he prefers to identify it with the Symplegades.) About the land of the Laestrygonians there is also much disagreement.

Circe's island is identified almost universally with Cape Circeo, but when we come to the Land of the Dead, we run into trouble. Is it Lake Averno in Italy, as some say, or is it beyond the Pillars of Hercules? Paul

Herrmann, in *Conquest by Man,* suggests that the dreary land of the Cimmerians (page 64) lies in the mists of northern Europe. As Herrmann says, some authorities place most of Odysseus' wanderings in the Atlantic, not the Mediterranean. Bradford and Berard disagree.

Except for the Land of the Dead, Bradford identifies every place-name in the Odyssey with a present-day spot in the Mediterranean. He puts the Sirens on the Galli Islands, the Isle of the Sun at Taormina (Sicily), and Calypso's Island on Malta. Like nearly everyone else he puts the land of the Phaeacians on Corfu, and Scylla and Charybdis in the Messina Strait. Surprisingly, even on Scylla and Charybdis there is not complete uniformity. Herrmann places them in the Strait of Gibraltar.

In Michel Gall's *The Voyages of Ulysses* there is an excellent map showing how Berard's and Bradford's voyages can be plotted. The similarities and differences are interesting. For the end papers of this book, however, we have chosen neither version. Instead we have avoided placing the marvelous sites at known places today. Since no one is really *sure,* we can continue to embroider the voyages with our own imaginations.

Michel Gall's book has superb color photographs that suggest the beauty and mystery of the *Odyssey.* If your library has a copy of this book, enjoy the pictures that bring scenes in the *Odyssey* to life. Louis Golding's *Good-bye to Ithaca* is a travel book dealing with many of the places mentioned in the *Odyssey*. The many pictures of the author's travels help a reader to see what the Mediterranean lands look like today.

If you are fascinated by the *Odyssey*, borrow Ernle Bradford's *Ulysses Found* from the library. His account is particularly impressive because he carefully sailed the route himself. Where the *Odyssey* describes the amount of time needed to get from place to place, he checked the distance in the light of sailing time required. He found, time and time again, that descriptions in the *Odyssey* tally with the descriptions in the *Admiralty Pilot,* a modern guide book for sailors. Though trees and certain other landmarks change over the centuries, other more lasting traces remain.

The ancients had their guide books too. During classical times, sailors borrowed or stole from each other these sailing helps called *periploi*. Perhaps the composer of the *Odyssey* had access to such a guide. At any rate, as Bradford says, "The *Odyssey* is the epic poem of a nation to whom navigation was all important."

Other sources you may enjoy are *Lands Beyond,* by L. Sprague de Camp and Willy Ley, and *The Wonder Book of Travellers' Tales,* by H. C. Adams. Both deal with the *Odyssey* and mention some of the guesses about the lands of the wanderings.

Many of the sources try to explain the marvels scientifically. To Michel Gall and to many others, Polyphemus is really a volcano. To Bradford, Polyphemus is just "a large and savage native." Bradford suggests that the name *Cyclopes* merely means "round faces." To Berard the single eye of Polyphemus may be a reference to ground-level craters that bubble with volcanic activity. Illustration 56 in *The Voyages of Ulysses* shows a picture of such a crater, and it *does* look like an eye. Robert Graves has another explanation. He says that the Cyclopes had an eye painted on their foreheads as a clan mark.

How did a legend like that of the Cyclopes originate? De Camp and Ley suggest that fossilized elephant skulls were often dug up and labeled the bones of giants. The nasal opening of such a skull looks like a single, round eye! And so we add another explanation to the legend of the Cyclopes. Who is right? We may never know, but our uncertainty need not interfere with our enjoyment of the *Odyssey*. Indeed the many guesses merely strengthen our interest in this great epic tale.

THE HISTORICAL BACKGROUND

Sometimes we tend to think of the rise of civilization as a constant moving forward. We may consider the ancient world quite barbaric in comparison with our own. But history shows us that the road isn't always upward. There are advances and declines in the rhythm of history.

Only a few years ago we knew very little about the second millennium (2000-1000 B.C.) This is the period of Stonehenge in England, of Akhenaton and Tutankhamen in Egypt, of Moses and Abraham in the Bible, and of the fall of Troy. Recent excavations, as we have seen, have clarified many problems and filled in many gaps.

This second millennium was a remarkable period in many ways, a kind of Golden Age. Surprisingly, it was often a time of peace. Trade routes expanded. Stable societies flourished for long periods. During long stretches of this era men could travel peacefully thousands of miles from home along the trade routes that linked the world together. In *Conquest of Man* Paul Herrmann tells the surprising story of these early trade routes along which amber and fur from northern Europe found their way to the Mediterranean in exchange for bronze objects.

During this period two great civilizations flourished in the Greek world: the Minoan (mi-NO-an) and the Mycenean (my-se-NEE-an). Both these civilizations contributed to the Greek civilization that flourished during the fifth century B.C.—the time of Pericles, Socrates, and Sophocles.

The Minoan civilization flourished on the island of Crete. This seafaring people produced a great, advanced civilization between 2000 and 1400 B.C. After 1900 B.C. the Myceneans, as they are now called, entered Greece and established important cities, many of which are mentioned by Homer. Close relationships were established between these two peoples. The more gentle, creative Minoans blended their culture with that of the more aggressive Myceneans. (In the legend of the

Minotaur, Greek mythology makes reference to the culture and civilization of Crete.) The Myceneans learned from both the Minoans and the Egyptians and forged a civilization that is depicted in the epics of Homer.

The Mycenean Greeks had their day in the sun and then began to decline. One reason may have been the invasion of Dorians, who entered the Greek cities from the north. The reasons are probably quite complex, but whatever they are, we do know that some time about 1200-1100 B.C. catastrophes overtook the great civilizations that had been established. The Hittite Empire collapsed. Egyptian power waned. There was destruction throughout the cities of Greece and Asia Minor. The Bronze Age was ending, and the Iron Age beginning. Old trade routes were disrupted. Once again civilization had to fight back from chaos to order.

The story of the second millennum is told with grace and charm in Geoffrey Bibby's *Four Thousand Years Ago*. Chapter 18 tells of the fall of Troy from the historical point of view.

THE WORLD OF ODYSSEUS

The world of Odysseus was quite different from that of Homer, for by Homer's time society had undergone many drastic upheavals. The society of Odysseus and Agamemnon was a society of kings and warriors, of aristocrats and noble families. We have many descriptions of this society in the *Odyssey* itself: customs in the land of the Phaeacians; the noblemen consuming the treasure of Odysseus.

It was a society very much concerned with honor and status. Trophies, gifts, and treasure were important in that society, and all of these were tied up with honor and status. Gift-giving was widespread, but those who gave always seemed to expect something in return. The treasure circulated from group to group, giving status to whoever had it. The custom of the feast went along with gift-giving. Both the *Odyssey* and the *Iliad* mention great feasts often.

In many ways it was a bloody, cruel society. Raids and piracy were frequent, a change from the more peaceful occupations of earlier generations. The motto was "To the victor belong the spoils," and the spoils included people. When a people were defeated in battle, often all the males were killed and the women led into slavery. The prophetess Cassandra, a Trojan princess, became a slave to Agamemnon after the fall of Troy.

It was not a democratic period. The common man had little say against the power of the aristocracy. When the common man speaks up in Homer, he is often rebuked and put in his place. A noble was concerned principally with only three groups: his class, his kin, and his household. He had no concern for society in general—for "mankind."

His class comprised all the nobility and royalty of equivalent rank elsewhere. Each leader felt keenly the obligations of his rank, and he was always concerned with appearances. Each leader was also closely attached to his relatives, or kin, though these might be separated in other lands. Finally, the leader was concerned with his household. The Greek word *oikos,* meaning "household," is the root of our words *economics* and *ecology.* The household included the family, the servants, the slaves, and all those closely associated with the group. As you see, the concept of a larger community had not developed too well during the time of Odysseus.

The position of women was generally an inferior one. Most women in the *Iliad* and the *Odyssey* are out of the mainstream of action. They do not play decisive roles. Even Helen is a passive spectator after the war has begun. The idea of deep romantic affection seems alien to these Homeric Greeks.

Agriculture was practiced, but the tending of cattle was more usual. The growing of crops became more important later as men tilled the soil more and more. Agriculture tends to require a more settled society, for men must stay on the land they cultivate.

M. I. Finley in *The World of Odysseus* examines all aspects of life in the Age of Heroes and brings this society to life for the reader. It was a society that glorified war and bloodshed, but it had developed many qualities that are admirable today. The friendships described in both the *Odyssey* and the *Iliad* seem, after nearly 2800 years, as fresh and appealing as they must have seemed to Homer's audience.

The Meaning of the Odyssey

"Be sure you are old when you drop anchor in Ithaca. Rich with the experiences you have gained upon your voyage, do not expect the island to give you riches. Ithaca has given you your wonderful voyage. Without Ithaca you would not have started." In these words the poet Constantine Cavafy sums up a philosophy of life and also, in a way, summarizes the *Odyssey* itself.

The *Odyssey* is more than an adventure yarn. In many ways it is a parable of life itself. Each man has an Odyssey that he must experience. He must strike out upon unknown seas and take a chance. He cannot live secure within a narrow space, locked in a closet of fear. He must go out on the seas and take a chance on life.

Though Ithaca is a distant and desirable destination, men must live on the voyage. Those who spend their lives looking only to the destination find that life has passed them by. Those who give up before they start never know what might have been. The philosopher Henri Bergson said, "I only know one way of finding out how far one can go, and that is by setting out and getting there." The *Odyssey* is the heroic story of a man who persisted and reached his Ithaca.

The very name *Odyssey* suggests a quest, a spiritual as well as a physical quest. The trials undergone by Odysseus were more than bouts with strange monsters. They were also the struggles of a man with himself.

GODS AND GODDESSES OF GREECE AND ROME

Greek Name	Roman Name	Identification*
Zeus	Jupiter	Supreme ruler of men and gods
Hera	Juno	Zeus's wife; guardian of women; queen of the gods
Poseidon	Neptune	God of the sea
Hades	Pluto	God of the dead
Persephone	Proserpina	Wife of Hades
Athena	Minerva	Goddess of wisdom
Ares	Mars	God of war
Artemis	Diana	Goddess of the moon
Apollo (sometimes Phoebus Apollo)	Apollo	God of the sun
Aphrodite	Venus	Goddess of love and beauty
Eros	Cupid	God of love
Hermes	Mercury	God of speed; messenger of the gods
Hephaestus	Vulcan	God of fire
Hestia	Vesta	Goddess of the hearth
Demeter	Ceres	Goddess of grain and harvests
Dionysus	Bacchus	God of wine

* The identifications are simplified. Actually, each god presided over many activities, not just one or two. Some functions overlapped. Several of the gods were worshiped under different names in different places. Too, the Greek and the Roman names do not correspond perfectly. Dionysus, for example, was in many ways a much more important god than Bacchus. However, the designations listed above are those most commonly accepted.

SUGGESTED ACTIVITIES

1. Make your own copy of the map that appears on pages 296 and 297 of this book. As Odysseus describes his wanderings, fill in the route as you go along.

One class made a game of the wanderings of Odysseus. They constructed a board with the map included in this book. They made counters for the players, and used a spinner with various numbers on the dial. They enjoyed setting up penalties and rewards. For example, if a counter landed on the island of the Cyclopes, the player had to go back a dozen spaces. On the other hand, if a counter landed on the island of the Phaeacians, the player was advanced directly to Ithaca. Try setting up a game yourself. You'll find the construction of the game almost as much fun as playing it. Decide your own penalties and rewards.

2. You will probably be interested in reading more about the Greek heroes mentioned, as well as the gods and goddesses. Several excellent books are available. Three of the best are the following:

Classic Myths	—	Gayley
Mythology	—	Bulfinch
Mythology	—	Hamilton

Your librarian will suggest other titles of interest.

3. If possible, try to obtain a modern translation of the *Iliad*. Read about Achilles, Agamemnon, Odysseus, Hector, and all the other great heroes. If you prefer, you may read the account of the *Iliad* as given in Gayley or some other book.

4. What happened after the close of the *Odyssey?* At least one poet tried to answer that question. Tennyson's *Ulysses* (the Latin name for Odysseus) is the story of Odysseus many years later. As he nears the end of his life, he yearns once again for the sea, for the adventures that he once had. He realizes that he may fail, but he is ready to take the chance. He feels that

260

the seeking is as important as the finding. The poem is reprinted below. Read it several times. Odysseus himself is speaking to his men. Decide for yourself what his attitude is. Your class may wish to make a more detailed study of the poem. If you do, you may wish to consider the questions at the end of the poem. This is a difficult poem. You will enjoy it best if you discuss it in class with the help of your teacher.

ULYSSES

It little profits that an idle king,
By this still hearth, among these barren crags,
Match'd with an aged wife, I mete and dole
Unequal laws unto a savage race,
That hoard, and sleep, and feed, and know not me.
I cannot rest from travel: I will drink
Life to the lees: all times I have enjoy'd
Greatly, have suffer'd greatly, both with those
That loved me, and alone; on shore, and when
Thro' scudding drifts the rainy Hyades
Vext the dim sea: I am become a name;
For always roaming with a hungry heart
Much have I seen and known; cities of men
And manners, climates, councils, governments,
Myself not least, but honour'd of them all;
And drunk delight of battle with my peers,
Far on the ringing plains of windy Troy.
I am a part of all that I have met;
Yet all experience is an arch wherethro'
Gleams that untravell'd world, whose margin fades
For ever and for ever when I move.
How dull it is to pause, to make an end,
To rust unburnish'd, not to shine in use!
As tho' to breathe were life. Life piled on life

Were all too little, and of one to me
Little remains: but every hour is saved
From that eternal silence, something more,
A bringer of new things; and vile it were
For some three suns to store and hoard myself,
And this gray spirit yearning in desire
To follow knowledge like a sinking star,
Beyond the utmost bound of human thought.
    This is my son, mine own Telemachus,
To whom I leave the sceptre and the isle—
Well-loved of me, discerning to fulfil
This labour, by slow prudence to make mild
A rugged people, and thro' soft degrees
Subdue them to the useful and the good.
Most blameless is he, centred in the sphere
Of common duties, decent not to fail
In offices of tenderness, and pay
Meet adoration to my household gods,
When I am gone. He works his work, I mine.
    There lies the port; the vessel puffs her sail:
There gloom the dark broad seas. My mariners,
Souls that have toil'd, and wrought, and thought with me—
That ever with a frolic welcome took
The thunder and the sunshine, and opposed
Free hearts, free foreheads—you and I are old;
Old age hath yet his honour and his toil;
Death closes all: but something ere the end,
Some work of noble note, may yet be done,
Not unbecoming men that strove with Gods.
The lights begin to twinkle from the rocks:
The long day wanes: the slow moon climbs: the deep
Moans round with many voices. Come, my friends,
'Tis not too late to seek a newer world.
Push off, and sitting well in order smite

The sounding furrows; for my purpose holds
To sail beyond the sunset, and the baths
Of all the western stars, until I die.
It may be that the gulfs will wash us down:
It may be we shall touch the Happy Isles,
And see the great Achilles, whom we knew.
Tho' much is taken, much abides; and tho'
We are not now that strength which in old days
Moved earth and heaven; that which we are, we are;
One equal temper of heroic hearts,
Made weak by time and fate, but strong in will
To strive, to seek, to find, and not to yield.

a. Is the Ulysses of Tennyson's poem the same man in spirit as the hero of the *Odyssey?*

b. Why does he yearn to leave Ithaca?

c. Where in the poem does Odysseus refer to his wanderings?

d. How does Odysseus differ from his son Telemachus? What does he mean by the words, "He works his work, I mine"?

e. For Odysseus the sea symbolizes mystery and adventure. Why?

f. Why does Odysseus scorn mere "living"?

g. Odysseus sees life as an unending quest for knowledge, adventure and new experience. Do you agree with him?

h. The last line is frequently quoted to describe persons of great courage and persistence. What does it mean? Does it apply to Odysseus?

i. What lines do you consider most beautiful?

5. Many common words are taken from Greek legends; for example, *herculean* to mean *of great strength.* Turn to page 229. What common words can you supply taken from the names of gods and goddesses?

6. People sometimes compare their own positions with those of characters in the *Odyssey*. Under what circumstances might a high school student say each of the following:

    a. I found myself between Scylla and Charybdis.

    b. I felt just like one of the Lotus-Eaters when I had to come home from camp.

    c. I went on an Odyssey.

Can you think of other expressions like these?

7. John Keats, like Tennyson, paid tribute to the epics of Homer. The following poem, *On First Looking into Chapman's Homer*, tells of Keats' feelings as he read the works of Homer for the first time—in Chapman's translation. Many of the lines are often quoted. Your class may wish to discuss the poem with your teacher's assistance.

Much have I travelled in the realms of gold
And many goodly states and kingdoms seen;
Round many western islands have I been
Which bards in fealty to Apollo hold.
Oft of one wide expanse had I been told
That deep-browed Homer ruled as his demesne;
Yet did I never breathe its pure serene
Till I heard Chapman speak out loud and bold:
Then felt I like some watcher of the skies
When a new planet swims into his ken;
Or like stout Cortez when with eagle eyes
He stared at the Pacific—and all his men
Looked at each other with a wild surmise—
Silent, upon a peak in Darien.

READING COMPREHENSION QUESTIONS

Chapter One

Complete each of the following statements by selecting one of the alternatives listed.

1. Calypso did not promise Odysseus ....
   (a. bread   b. a safe return   c. a favorable wind).
2. At Calypso's first offer Odysseus was ....
   (a. happy   b. weeping   c. distrustful).
3. Odysseus set out to build a ....
   (a. raft   b. small boat   c. houseboat).
4. "The Seven Sisters" is another name for ....
   (a. The Pleiades   b. The Bear   c. The Dipper).
5. The direction he wished to hold to was ....
   (a. west   b. north   c. east).
6. .... aroused the sea against Odysseus.
   (a. Poseidon   b. Athena   c. Calypso).
7. Odysseus came to .... (a. his own island
   b. the land of the Phaeacians   c. Poseidon's palaces).
8. Ino provided Odysseus with ....
   (a. a new sail   b. a scarf   c. a magic ring).
9. Ino was .... (a. a goddess of the sea
   b. the same as Athena   c. queen of the Phaeacians).
10. The coastline was dangerous because of ....
    (a. whirlpools   b. rocks   c. quicksands).

Chapter Two

Tell whether each of the following statements is true or false.

1. Athena spoke to Nausicaa in the guise of a close friend.
2. Nausicaa was not related to Arete.
3. Odysseus was awakened by the noise made by the girls.

265

4. Nausicaa asked her father for a wagon to take clothes out for laundering.
5. Nausicaa ran away at the sight of Odysseus.
6. Nausicaa admitted freely that she was the daughter of the king.
7. Odysseus followed Nausicaa's wagon all the way into the city.
8. Nausicaa thought Odysseus was the kind of person she'd like to marry.
9. Odysseus showed little respect for Nausicaa when he spoke to her.
10. Nausicaa advised Odysseus to go directly to her father for aid.

Chapter Three

Complete the following paragraph by selecting for each number an alternative listed below. There are several extra choices. You may use a choice more than once.

Alcinous	Ogygia
Arete	an old man
Athena	Poseidon
Calypso	a servant
a child	a young woman
Nausicaa	Zeus

Odysseus waited while ....1.... returned to the city. At last he set out himself. ....2.... made him invisible so that he would not be addressed by any of the Phaeacians. Near the city ....3.... appeared to him in the likeness of ....4.... Then Odysseus reached the palace of ....5.... He immediately entered and threw himself at the feet of ....6.... ....7.... spoke up and urged ....8.... to be courteous. Odysseus explained that he had come from ....9...., home of ....10....

Chapter Four

Complete each of the following statements.
1. . . . . urged the Phaeacians to shower Odysseus with gifts.
2. The minstrel had lost . . . .
3. Alcinous promised Odysseus a sturdy ship to . . . .
4. Demodocus sang the story of the famous quarrel between Achilles and . . . .
5. During this recital . . . . wept.
6. Odysseus felt that . . . . had insulted him.
7. Odysseus showed his great skill in . . . .
8. . . . . disguised herself as the referee.
9. . . . . reminded Odysseus that he owed his life to her.
10. . . . . was the only one who noticed Odysseus' weeping.

Chapter Five

Match items in Column B with those in Column A. There will be one left over in Column B.

A	B
1. Alcinous	A. Odysseus' father
2. Ciconians	B. King of the Phaeacians
3. Cyclopes	C. Home of Odysseus
4. Ithaca	D. Taunted Polyphemus
5. Laertes	E. Their city attacked by Odysseus
6. Lotus-Eaters	F. Was blinded
7. No-man	G. Forgot the past
8. Odysseus	H. Father of Polyphemus
9. Polyphemus	I. Odysseus' assumed name
10. Poseidon	J. Odysseus' friend among the gods
	K. Monsters

Chapter Six

Complete each of the following statements by selecting one of the alternatives listed.

1. .... gave Odysseus the bag of winds.
   (a. Aeolus   b. Eurylochus   c. Circe)
2. .... caused the men to open the bag of winds.
   (a. Cruelty   b. Wisdom   c. Greed)
3. On his second return to Aeolia, Odysseus was ....
   (a. treated like a king   b. sent out angrily   c. made captive)
4. Odysseus lost .... in the land of the Laestrygonians.
   (a. all of his men   b. all of his ships but one   c. one of his ships)
5. The Laestrygonians were ....
   (a. friendly   b. dwarfs   c. giants)
6. Circe turned the men into ....
   (a. lions   b. wolves   c. pigs)
7. Odysseus was assisted by ....
   (a. Eurylochus   b. Elpenor   c. Hermes)
8. Circe enchanted her captives by means of a ....
   and a rod. (a. magic carpet   b. ring   c. drug)
9. Circe told Odysseus he'd have to visit the land of the dead
   to consult .... (a. Pluto   b. Persephone   c. Tiresias)
10. Before the men left, ... was killed.
    (a. Tiresias   b. Elpenor   c. Eurylochus).

Chapter Seven

Match items in Column B with those in Column A. There will be one left over in Column B.

A	B
1. Achilles	A. Seer and prophet for Odysseus
2. Agamemnon	B. Urged Odysseus to finish his tale
3. Ajax	C. Told of his murder by his wife
4. Alcinous	D. Was eager for news of his son Neoptolemus
5. Hercules	
6. Minos	E. Refused to speak to Odysseus
7. Sisyphus	F. Was continually devoured by vultures
8. Tantalus	G. Fell from a roof and was killed
9. Tiresias	H. Suffered thirst while surrounded by water
10. Tityus	
	I. Judge of the dead
	J. Once captured the watchdog of Hades
	K. Rolled a stone vainly up a hill

Chapter Eight

Match items in Column B with those in Column A. There will be one left over in Column B.

A	B
1. Aeaea	A. Gave Odysseus good advice
2. Argo	B. Circe's island
3. Cattle of the Sun	C. God of the Sun
4. Charybdis	D. Famous ship
5. Circe ..	E. Six-headed monster
6. Jason	F. Whirlpool
7. Scylla	G. Isle of the Sun
8. Sirens	H. Famous Greek hero

9. Trinacria   I. Slain by Odysseus' men
10. Zeus   J. Struck Odysseus' ship with thunder-
                        bolt
                    K. Sang a song of enchantment

Chapter Nine

Tell whether each statement is true or false.
1. Odysseus left the land of the Phaeacians at sunrise.
2. The Phaeacians gave Odysseus many gifts.
3. The Phaeacians put Odysseus ashore while he was still asleep.
4. Poseidon sought vengeance upon the Phaeacians because they had taken Odysseus home.
5. Zeus was angry with Poseidon and refused to let him do what he wished.
6. Odysseus realized at once when he awoke that he was in Ithaca.
7. The first one to speak to Odysseus in Ithaca was Athena.
8. Athena admired Odysseus for his shrewdness and cunning.
9. Athena sent Odysseus at once to the palace.
10. Athena transformed Odysseus into a ragged old man.

Chapter Ten

Complete the following paragraph by selecting for each number an alternative listed below. There are several extra choices. You may use a choice more than once.

bed	disbelieved	Ithaca	the servants
believed	Egypt	the land of the Phaeacians	the suitors
cloak	Eumaeus	Odysseus	the Trojan
Crete	the herdsmen	Penelope	War

Odysseus arrived at the hut of ....1...., the swineherd. He found the swineherd lamenting the absence of ....2.... and cursing the presence of ....3.... Odysseus insisted that he had news of ....4.... The swineherd ....5.... the news. In the tale that he made up Odysseus insisted that he was a native of ....6.... and that he had been taken captive in ....7.... The swineherd declared that ....8.... was extremely anxious for news of her husband. To get a ....9.... for sleeping, Odysseus told a tall story about his own experiences in ....10....

Chapter Eleven

Complete each of the following statements.

1. .... was the name of Telemachus' host in Sparta.
2. His wife was the famous ....
3. .... went to Sparta to induce Telemachus to return.
4. Before Telemachus left, he saw a good omen, which was ....
5. .... escorted Telemachus back home.
6. Eumaeus told Odysseus about Odysseus' father, whose name was ....
7. Eumaeus told Odysseus that his own birthplace was ......
8. He had been kidnaped by some .... traders.
9. When Telemachus arrived, he saw another good omen, which was ....
10. The omen was interpreted favorably by the prophet ....

Chapter Twelve

Complete each of the following statements by selecting one of the alternatives listed.

1. The dogs did not bark at the arrival of................
   (a. Odysseus   b. Telemachus   c. Antinous).
2. When Telemachus entered, he treated the stranger ....
   (a. rudely   b. courteously   c. indifferently).
3. Telemachus promised the supposed stranger ....
   (a. a two-edged sword   b. nothing   c. a gold ring).

4. Telemachus sent Eumaeus with news of his return to ......
(a. Laertes   b. Antinous   c. Penelope).
5. .... advised Odysseus to reveal himself to his son.
(a. Athena   b. Eumaeus   c. Amphinomus)
6. When Telemachus saw the change in the stranger, he was
.... (a. amused   b. frightened   c. bored).
7. When Telemachus heard that his father intended to slay all
the suitors without a large number of assistants, he was
.... (a. made angry   b. amazed   c. pleased).
8. Odysseus declared he'd go to the city looking like ....
(a. himself   b. a beggar   c. a warrior).
9. Odysseus planned to hide away all the ....
(a. food   b. armor   c. rich clothing).
10. Among the suitors .... advised the immediate killing
of Telemachus. (a. Antinous   b. Eurymachus   c. Amphinomus)

Chapter Thirteen

Match items in Column B with those in Column A. There
will be one left over in Column B.

	A	B
1.	Antinous	A. Told his mother of his travels
2.	Argus	B. Led Odysseus to the city
3.	Eumaeus	C. Old nurse
4.	Eurycleia	D. Rejoiced at Telemachus' sneeze
5.	Medon	E. Died after seeing his master
6.	Melanthius	F. Made prophecy about return of Mene-
7.	Menelaus	laus
8.	Odysseus	G. Called Eumaeus "king of the pigs"
9.	Penelope	H. Threw a footstool at Odysseus
10.	Telemachus	I. The herald
		J. Told Telemachus Calypso had captured Odysseus
		K. Asked Antinous for charity

Chapter Fourteen

Complete each of the following statements.
1. Another beggar named .... appeared to challenge Odysseus.
2. .... helped to arrange the fight between the two.
3. He promised that the winner would have the privilege of ....
4. .... promised fair play for Odysseus.
5. When Irus saw Odysseus' powerful build, he was ....
6. Odysseus overcame the beggar by ....
7. Odysseus took the beggar to .... where he propped him up.
8. Odysseus advised .... to leave the other suitors.
9. .... scolded Telemachus and the suitors for their treatment of Odysseus.
10. ...., one of the handmaidens, abused Odysseus with bitter words.

Chapter Fifteen

Tell whether each statement is true or false.
1. Telemachus hid away all the armor in the storeroom.
2. Penelope scolded her servant for abusing Odysseus.
3. Odysseus told Penelope the truth in everything.
4. Penelope was eager to finish the robe she was weaving.
5. Penelope tested the stranger by asking what clothes Odysseus had been wearing.
6. Odysseus promised that Odysseus would soon be back in Ithaca.
7. Eurycleia did not think that the stranger looked like Odysseus.
8. Odysseus had received in battle the scar by which he was recognized.
9. Odysseus allowed Eurycleia to tell Penelope, but no one else.
10. In Penelope's dream the eagle killed the palace geese.

Chapter Sixteen

Complete each of the following statements by selecting one of the alternatives listed.

1. Odysseus feared that if he slew the suitors a ....
would follow. (a. plague   b. feud   c. storm)

2. Penelope prayed to .... for merciful death.
(a. Athena   b. Zeus   c. Artemis)

3. .... sent forth a thunderclap. (a. Athena
b. Zeus   c. Artemis)

4. .... once again insulted Odysseus. (a. Irus
b. Melanthius   c. Philoetius)

5. .... urged the other suitors to drop the plan to kill
Telemachus. (a. Antinous   b. Ctesippus   c. Amphinomus)

6. .... prophesied doom for the suitors. (a. Agelaus
b. Theoclymenus   c. Melanthius)

7. .... threw an ox's hoof at Odysseus. (a. Ctesippus
b. Melanthius   c. Amphinomus)

8. .... showed his loyalty to Odysseus. (a. Antinous
b. Philoetius   c. Agelaus)

9. Telemachus became .... at the treatment of Odysseus.
(a. angry   b. grateful   c. indifferent)

10. If a bird flew on the ...., the omen was considered
unlucky. (a. north   b. left   c. right)

Chapter Seventeen

Complete the following paragraph by selecting for each number an alternative listed below. There are several extra choices. You may use a choice more than once.

Antinous	Eurymachus	Mycene	Philoetius
Eumaeus	King Echetus	Odysseus	Pylos
Eurycleia	Leiodes	Penelope	Telemachus

....1.... proposed that the suitors try to bend the great
bow ....2.... ....3.... and ....4.... wept when they
saw the bow. ....5.... scolded them for their weeping. The
first one to try to bend the bow was ....6.... ....7....
nodded at him not to try a fourth time to bend it. Among the
suitors ....8.... was first to try. ....9.... shocked the
suitors by asking for a chance to try the bow. ....10.... insisted at once that he be allowed to try.

Chapter Eighteen

Match items in Column B with those in Column A. There
will be one left over in Column B.

A	B
1. Agelaus	A. Spared the life of the herald
2. Amphinomus	B. First to be slain
3. Antinous	C. Second to die
4. Athena	D. Slain by Telemachus
5. Eumaeus	E. Brought arms to the suitors
6. Eurycleia	F. Bound Melanthius
7. Eurymachus	G. Was ordered to fumigate the palace
8. Melanthius	H. Had neglected to close the storeroom
9. Odysseus	door
10. Philoetius	I. Urged six suitors to attack Odysseus
	J. Slew Ctesippus
	K. Took likeness of Mentor

Chapter Nineteen

Tell whether each statement is true or false.
1. Penelope immediately believed the news of Odysseus' return.
2. Telemachus broke the news of Odysseus' return to Penelope.
3. Penelope thought the gods had slain the suitors.

4. When Penelope met Odysseus, she rushed into his arms at once.
5. Telemachus scolded Penelope for her actions.
6. Odysseus feared the vengeance of the families of the suitors.
7. People outside the palace thought Penelope had married at last.
8. Odysseus proved his identity by describing his bed.
9. The bed was light and easily carried.
10. Odysseus declared his intentions of visiting Laertes.

Chapter Twenty

Complete each of the following statements.
1. Odysseus went to the farm of Laertes and found him in ....
2. Odysseus couldn't resist playing a prank on his father. Accordingly, he declared that his name was ....
3. Laertes was certain that .... had died.
4. Odysseus proved his identity by describing ....
5. .... made Laertes taller and more majestic to look at.
6. The families of the suitors had gathered under the leadership of ....
7. The herald .... advised the families not to attack Odysseus.
8. .... slew the father of Antinous.
9. When .... spoke, the men stopped fighting.
10. Zeus sent forth .... as a warning to stop the battle.

ENRICHING YOUR READING

Chapter One

1. Why was Odysseus reluctant, at first, to believe Calypso?
2. Calypso declared, "Surely, she is not more beautiful than I?" How did Odysseus, in his reply, justify his reputation for cleverness?
3. The Bear, our Big Dipper, is a far northern star group. In which direction would Odysseus have been moving if he had kept the Bear on his right? If he had kept it in front of him? Directly in back of him? Why did ancient mariners have to rely so completely upon the stars?
4. To the ancient Greeks, whose livelihood and wealth depended upon the sea, storms and shipwrecks were major calamities. There were no Coast Guard Cutters to pick up survivors. How does this chapter suggest the utter helplessness of men before the fury of the storm?
5. How did Odysseus display typical caution in the episode of the scarf?
6. As far as Odysseus is concerned, the god Poseidon is the villain of the story. (a) How does the inclusion of such a powerful villain add interest to the story? (b) How does it add to Odysseus' prowess? (c) What hint is given that even Poseidon must bow to the will of the Fates?
7. If Poseidon is the villain of the story, then Athena is Odysseus' guardian angel. She plays an important part in the story. She keeps reappearing. Do you like her better than Poseidon? Why?

Chapter Two

1. Why did not Athena send Odysseus directly into the city? Why did she induce Nausicaa to meet Odysseus first?

2. We form our impressions of people in many ways; for example, by what they say and do, by their appearance, by their reputation, and by the opinions of other people. How is our opinion of Odysseus raised by the way Arete, Alcinous, and Athena treat him?

3. In what ways is Nausicaa's character revealed for us? How does she resemble girls of today?

4. The *Odyssey* describes events that are distant from us more than 3000 years. Yet many lines could have been written yesterday. As you read the *Odyssey,* look for human characteristics and traits that are as typical today as they were thirty centuries ago. What examples have you noticed thus far?

5. Odysseus is thrust into many strange situations in the book; yet he always manages to keep his wits about him. How did he show his resourcefulness in his meeting with Nausicaa?

6. Why didn't Nausicaa take Odysseus directly into the city with her?

Chapter Three

1. Why did Nausicaa tell Odysseus to beg assistance first of the queen, rather than of the king?

2. Are there signs that Alcinous ruled the Phaeacians democratically rather than cruelly? Is the reader favorably impressed with Alcinous? Why?

3. The Phaeacians were truly "isolationists." Do you know the meaning of the word? How does it apply to them?

4. Arete showed that she was a good detective. How? In his reply how did Odysseus protect Nausicaa? What good quality does that reveal in him?

5. Odysseus tells, in this chapter, part of the story of his wanderings. Can you retell it?

6. What promise made to Odysseus pleased him?

Chapter Four

1. Surely Arete, Alcinous, and all the other Phaeacians were burning up with curiosity to know where Odysseus came from. (Wouldn't you have been?) Yet they refrained from asking him for a whole day. Why did they wait?

2. According to legend, Homer, the author of the *Odyssey,* was a blind poet. Who in this chapter most resembles Homer? What was his job at the banquet?

3. Certainly the ancient Greeks loved wining and dining. The *Odyssey* is filled with feasts, descriptions of banquets, the joy of good eating. How does this chapter help prove that statement?

4. (a) Why did the two young men taunt Odysseus? Were they intentionally unpleasant? (b) How did Odysseus reply to them? (c) Does his success help build up our own picture of him? How?

5. (a) How did Alcinous show his pride in his country and yet avoid insulting Odysseus? (b) What responsibilities did a host have toward his guest in those days?

6. Nausicaa appears in this chapter for the last time. In her speech is there any hint of her feelings toward Odysseus? Why could not Odysseus have stayed to marry her?

7. How did Alcinous at last ask Odysseus the story of his life? What excuse did he seize upon?

8. Notice the dramatic build-up here. The minstrel sings about Troy, the Greeks, and great Odysseus himself. The audience is keyed up about the Trojan War. Then Alcinous turns to the stranger and asks his name. What do you suppose happened when the stranger said, "I am Odysseus, son of Laertes"?

Chapter Five

1. Was Odysseus fair in his attack on the Ciconians? What does that tell us about war in those days?

2. As the wandering of Odysseus goes on, he loses more and more men. The episode with the Ciconians is just a foretaste of what is to come. In almost every case Odysseus or the men seem to be responsible for their destruction. How did they bring on their own difficulties in the land of the Ciconians?

3. How much navigation do you know? Why did Odysseus and his men have to lower the sails in the storm?

4. Even today the southern coast of Greece is very dangerous for smaller craft. Look at the map. Can you see why Odysseus could have come home quickly and safely if he had been able to pass southern Greece without harm?

5. The episode of the Cyclops builds up suspense at once. This time it is Odysseus who brings on misfortune. What steps did Odysseus fortunately take in advance, steps that led to his freedom eventually and to the safety of his ships?

6. At several points Odysseus outsmarted the monster. Can you find them?

7. Why didn't Odysseus kill the monster while he slept? What plan did he devise?

8. How did the Cyclops' gift to Odysseus show the monster's grim sense of humor?

9. Did you have any sympathy for the Cyclops? Why or why not?

10. How did Odysseus' desire to get in the last word almost prove his undoing?

11. This is an important episode, because forever after Poseidon is bitter toward Odysseus. Why?

Chapter Six

1. (a) Why was Aeolus able to harness all the winds for Odysseus? (b) Look up *aeolian* harp in a good dictionary.

How did it get its name? (c) Why was Aeolus so bitter toward Odysseus on his second visit?

2. How did the men's own foolishness bring disaster? On what previous occasion did stupidity bring trouble?

3. (a) The Laestrygonians accounted for more of Odysseus' men than did all the other monsters combined. How did Odysseus escape? (b) On what previous occasions did he show foresight and caution?

4. (a) How do you suppose stories of monsters like the Laestrygonians originated? (b) Why did travelers to distant lands feel free to enrich their accounts with vivid (and often untrue) details? (c) Suppose in our own day a rocket traveler to another planet came back with a fantastic story of his adventures. How would you accept them? Why?

5. (a) In the discussion about going to Circe's house, Eurylochus disagreed violently with Odysseus. What does this dispute add to the story? (b) Do you like Eurylochus? (c) Was he right or wrong?

6. Though he suffered much, Odysseus was under the protection of the gods at really crucial moments. What proof have we in this chapter?

7. (a) Is Circe a likable personality? (b) How did she help Odysseus?

8. Look at your map on the inside cover. The ancients believed that the stream of Ocean surrounded the entire world, and that on the other side was the Land of the Dead. Some travelers must have sailed through the Straits of Gibraltar into the Atlantic Ocean—for indeed the oceans do surround all the lands, though not in the way the Greeks thought. Look at a present-day map of the Mediterranean. If Odysseus did sail beyond Gibraltar, how far did he travel away from his home island Ithaca?

9. (a) How did the men take the news of their trip to the Land of the Dead? (b) Why were they so disturbed?

Chapter Seven

1. How did Elpenor manage to get to the Land of the Dead before Odysseus? (Incidentally, this is often quoted as a Homeric joke.)
2. How did the shades manage to talk, though they were but shadows?
3. What prophecies did Tiresias make?
4. Why was Odysseus surprised to find his mother there?
5. Odysseus proves over and over again in the story that he is a supreme story-teller. He knows how to arouse his listeners and make them beg for more. (a) Knowing this, can you tell why Odysseus stopped his story in the middle and told the Phaeacians, "It is time for sleep"? (b) What would you have done in their place? (c) What did the Phaeacians do? (Notice, too, that this device reminds the readers that Odysseus is telling this story to Alcinous and the rest.)
6. As you read this section about the Greek heroes, refer to the Trojan War on page 223 for the complete story.
7. The stories of the Greek heroes were made into great plays by the Greek writers of tragedy: Aeschylus, Sophocles, and Euripides. Perhaps someone in the class will be able to find out something about Aeschylus' *Agamemnon,* for example.
8. (a) From the description given here can you tell something about the Greek version of a life after death? (b) Did the dead keep their human qualities and failings? (Reread the description of Ajax's attitude toward Odysseus, who had once bested him in a contest.) (c) What were some of the punishments meted out in Hades?
9. Why did Odysseus leave in haste?

Chapter Eight

1. How did Odysseus fulfill his promise to Elpenor?
2. How did Circe show her own sense of humor?

3. A *dilemma* is a situation involving a choice between two alternatives, both unpleasant. How was Odysseus faced with a dilemma on his homeward journey?
4. Reference is made by Circe to the voyage of the Argo under Jason. In one of the books suggested on page 230, look up the story of the Argonauts. You will become acquainted with the enchantress Medea, the Golden Fleece, the Dragon's Teeth, and other colorful ingredients of a wonderful legend.
5. (a) Why was it strategically wiser to choose Scylla, horrible though she was? (b) Why could not Odysseus fight back? (c) Why did he not tell his men in advance about Scylla?
6. Why did Odysseus want to hear the Siren song himself?
7. Readers sometimes feel that "the cards were stacked" against Odysseus, that disaster would have come to him no matter what he did. How is that feeling borne out in the episode of the cattle of the Sun?
8. (a) On Odysseus' way with his men, Scylla was the better risk; on his way back alone, Charybdis was the better risk. Why? (b) How did Odysseus save himself from the whirlpool?

Chapter Nine

1. What effect did Odysseus' tale have on his listeners?
2. (a) Why was Poseidon angry with the Phaeacians? (b) How did he propose to avenge himself?
3. (a) Why did not Odysseus recognize Ithaca at once? (b) How did Athena do Odysseus a good turn by insisting he act slowly and cautiously?
4. (a) How did Athena show her affection for Odysseus? (b) Why did she like him so much?
5. As several previous questions have indicated, *Fate* in the *Odyssey* is all-powerful. Even Poseidon admits several times that he can make matters uncomfortable for Odysseus, but he cannot stop him from returning. How does the fol-

lowing speech of Athena's bear out the idea of all-powerful fate?

"I always knew that you would return at last, although you would lose all your comrades."

6. Why did Athena transform Odysseus into an old man?

Chapter Ten

1. Beginning with this chapter Odysseus meets more and more Ithacans. Some are faithful and friendly; others are traitorous and cruel. Eumaeus is first. How would you classify him?
2. We have noticed before that Odysseus loves to tell stories. (a) What yarn did he tell Eumaeus? (b) How did he bring the name of Odysseus into it?
3. How did Odysseus get a cloak for himself by telling a clever story?
4. This chapter has a fine bit of humor. Odysseus declares emphatically, "I hate like the gates of Hades the man who is forced by poverty to tell a lie." Eumaeus declares, "Now, old man, tell me about yourself." How does Odysseus' reply show the author's sense of humor?
5. How did Eumaeus show his fine character in his treatment of Odysseus?
6. Eumaeus made what modern readers would call a "wisecrack." He said, "How did the sailors bring you to Ithaca? I don't imagine you walked here." How might a modern young man in like manner greet a new arrival at a party?

Chapter Eleven

1. (a) Why did Athena persuade Telemachus to go home at once? (b) How did she instruct him to avoid the ambush?
2. What does this chapter tell the reader about the Greek belief in omens and prophecies?

3. How did Odysseus test Eumaeus?
4. Why could not Telemachus invite guests to his own house?
5. Why did Telemachus return to the city by way of Eumaeus' hut?

Chapter Twelve

1. Why did not the dogs bark when Telemachus approached?
2. (a) How did Eumaeus greet Telemachus? (b) What does this tell us about Telemachus?
3. How did Telemachus show consideration for his mother Penelope?
4. (a) Why hadn't Telemachus attacked the suitors and thrust them from his house? (b) On the other hand, why hadn't the suitors slain Telemachus and forced Penelope to choose?
5. Notice how many times Eumaeus and Telemachus refer to the absent Odysseus. How does such frequent mention arouse suspense and interest?
6. Why was Telemachus at first doubtful that this was indeed his father?
7. What plans did Odysseus make for the attack on the suitors?
8. This chapter gives the readers the first glimpse of the suitors. Several are mentioned by name; each one is distinguished from the others. Antinous, for example, is the bullying ringleader, vain and cunning. As you read, form your impressions of Antinous, Eurymachus, Amphinomus, and the rest. Of the three suitors mentioned which is the hypocrite? (Look up the meaning of the word *hypocrite* if you are doubtful.)

Chapter Thirteen

1. Each successive chapter suggests the rising excitement of the return. Odysseus meets the swineherd, then Telemachus. In this chapter he returns to his home and sees the trouble

at first hand. The meeting with Penelope is delayed still longer. Why?

2. (a) What very human scene between Penelope and Telemachus is described in this chapter? (b) Is 't effective? (c) Could it happen as readily today as 3000 years ago?

3. The reader has learned about Penelope from many persons in the *Odyssey*. In this chapter Penelope actually appears. (a) What impression does the reader have of her? (b) A loyal wife today is sometimes called a "Penelope." Why?

4. (a) In what manner did Melanthius speak to Odysseus? (b) Why didn't Odysseus kill him on the spot?

5. One of the most famous episodes in the *Odyssey* is a brief one—the story of Odysseus' meeting with his faithful old dog Argus. (a) Why is the scene so effective? (b) How do we know that Odysseus has been deeply touched?

6. Why was it necessary for Odysseus to delay for a while vengeance upon the suitors?

7. How did the suitors prove to Odysseus that they merited destruction?

8. Why was Penelope eager to speak to the old beggar?

Chapter Fifteen

1. Why did Odysseus store away the arms?

2. (a) Why did Penelope confide in Odysseus? (b) What news was she hoping for? (c) Why did she seem to disbelieve the good news about her husband?

3. Why was "the old beggar" able to give Penelope so many accurate details about his meeting with Odysseus many years before?

4. (a) Why did Odysseus insist upon Eurycleia to bathe him? (b) Why did he insist that Eurycleia not tell Penelope about the scar?

5. Why did Odysseus tell Penelope to go ahead with the contest?

Chapter Sixteen

1. Why was Odysseus worried about the outcome of the coming battle?
2. What new ally to Odysseus' cause arrived in this chapter?
3. How did the gods, by omens on several occasions, help Odysseus' cause?
4. Theoclymenus gave the suitors a hint of threatening disaster. Why didn't they heed him?

Chapter Seventeen

1. Why did Odysseus hint that Telemachus should not try the bow a fourth time?
2. (a) How did Odysseus assure himself of his men's loyalty? (b) How did he prove his identity?
3. (a) How did Antinous seek to put off the contest of the great bow? (b) How did the suitors react to Odysseus' offer to try the bow? Why?
4. Why did Odysseus have the doors locked?
5. One of the suitors says, "Little good he'll ever get out of stretching that bow." What secret, unknown to the suitor, gives the reader a hint that the statement is wrong?
6. Some readers feel that the ending of this chapter is one of the most exciting and dramatic in the book. Do you agree?

Chapter Eighteen

1. (a) Why did Odysseus slay Antinous first? (b) Was he justified in killing him without warning?
2. Revenge is often called a primitive and an uncivilized emotion. (a) Do you feel that revenge is justified here? (b) Is it ever justified? (c) What is the religious attitude toward revenge?
3. Should Odysseus have spared some of the suitors, or was he right in killing all?

4. How did Melanthius's treachery almost cause the destruc tion of Odysseus' plans?
5. Was the battle won entirely by the strength of Odysseus and his men? Explain.
6. Who were saved? Why?
7. Why was the possible feud almost as dangerous as the attack upon the suitors?
8. (a) What examples of primitive cruelty were shown in the treatment of Melanthius and the disloyal women? (b) How did Nazism and Fascism actually outdo these examples of barbarity during World War II? (c) How does democracy plan to safeguard its citizens against such cruelty?

Chapter Nineteen

1. (a) Odysseus had been away for twenty years. Yet when Penelope was told Odysseus had returned, she hesitated about going to him. Why? (b) Had she reason for her hesitation?
2. (a) How did Penelope lay a trap to discover whether the stranger was indeed Odysseus? (b) Why did she consider his explanation satisfactory proof?
3. Whom did Odysseus wish to see next?

Chapter Twenty

1. How did Odysseus show that, even with his father, he could not resist the opportunity to tell a story?
2. Is Laertes a likable person? Why?
3. Why did the townsmen rise against Odysseus?
4. Who finally settled the feud?
5. (a) Do you consider the ending fitting? (b) What probably happened next? (c) Was Odysseus happy to be home at last, away from the uncertain sea? (Read Lord Tennyson's version of Odysseus' life as an old man on page 231.)

6. The *Odyssey* has often been called the world's greatest adventure story. It has much action, interesting characters, suspense, imagination, monsters, gods and goddesses, even humor. Can you, in summing up, prove the statement by referring frequently to the book?

THE ODYSSEY

Comprehensive Examination A

Thirty Minutes

I. Testing for Information (40 points)

A. Identify these important characters in the "Odyssey" by matching the numbers in column A with the proper letters in column B:

A	B
1. Polyphemus	a. most beautiful of women
2. Poseidon	b. one-eyed monster
3. Eumaeus	c. enemy of Odysseus
4. Circe	d. turned men to swine
5. Helen of Troy	e. faithful friend of Odysseus

B. Complete the following sentences with the correct word:

1. .... went to Sparta to seek news of Odysseus.
2. .... was the monster who devoured half a dozen men at a time.
3. Nausicaa lived in the land of ....
4. .... told Odysseus to assume the disguise of an old man.
5. .... refused to accept the offers of men who wanted to marry her.

C. Make the choice ("a", "b", or "c") which will complete the following statements correctly:

1. The husband of Helen of Troy was: a. Menelaus; b. Priam; c. Agamemnon.
2. Polyphemus was the son of: a. Odysseus; b. Athena; c. Poseidon.

3. The land of the dead was called: a. Ithaca; b. Hades; c. Phaeacia.
4. The sacred cattle belonged to the: a. God of the Sun; b. God of the Underworld; c. God of the Sea.
5. Irresistible singers were the: a. Lotus-Eaters; b. Ciconians; c. Sirens.
6. Odysseus was held captive by: a. Calypso; b. Athena; c. Nausicaa.
7. Prophecies were made by: a. Eurylochus; b. Tiresias; c. Jason.
8. The home of Odysseus was the island of: a. Crete; b. Ithaca; c. Trinacria.
9. When Odysseus left for the Trojan War, Telemachus was a: a. baby; b. old man; c. young man.
10. The poet who composed the *Odyssey* is named: a. Homer; b. Odysseus; c. Athena.

II. Testing Vocabulary (40 points)

A. Choose the best meaning for each of the following words from the five choices given:
1. SEER   a. burn; b. prophet; c. warrior; d. friend; e. sailor
2. TANTALIZE   a. proclaim; b. create; c. fear; d. remain; e. tease
3. HERDSMAN   a. shepherd; b. fighter; c. ghost; d. wanderer; e. enemy
4. COUNSELOR   a. bookkeeper; b. farmer; c. adviser; d. terror; e. complainer
5. TREACHEROUS   a. lifeless; b. colored; c. satisfied; d. traitorous; e. outraged

B. Place the following words from the story you have just read in the proper sentences:
   a. taunt; b. omen; c. sorceress; d. feud; e. wrath
1. Circe was a .... who tricked Odysseus' men.
2. The appearance of Athena was a good ....
3. Odysseus wanted to .... Polyphemus.

4. The .... of Poseidon was turned against Odysseus.

5. With the ending of the ...., peace prevailed.

C. Match the words in column A with those terms in column B which mean the same, or nearly the same:

A	B
1. staunch	a. singer
2. dismay	b. disappointment
3. disheveled	c. firm
4. impress	d. unkempt
5. minstrel	e. make an impression

D. Match the words in column A with those terms in column B which mean the opposite, or nearly the opposite:

A	B
1. abundance	a. leisure activities
2. chores	b. conscious state
3. stupor	c. lavishly
4. restrain	d. scarcity
5. skimpily	e. encourage

III. Testing Understanding (20 points)

A. Rearrange the following events as they happen in the story:

1. Odysseus hears the Sirens.
2. Odysseus meets Scylla.
3. Odysseus is recognized by his old nurse.
4. Odysseus is reunited with Penelope.
5. The suitors are punished.

B. Complete the following statements by making the proper choice:

1. Another suitable title for this story might be: a. The Ten-Year Journey; b. Gods and Goddesses; c. Olden Times.

2. Penelope is shown to be: a. faithful; b. faithless; c. thoughtless.
3. The ancient Greeks believed that the gods: a. often opposed each other; b. were always in agreement; c. lived in Hades.
4. Among the sports favored by the Greeks were hurling the javelin and: a. football; b. baseball; c. wrestling.
5. Although he had many virtues, Odysseus is: a. cowardly; b. boastful; c. disloyal.

Comprehensive Examination B

Thirty Minutes

I. Testing for Information (40 points)

A. Identify these important characters in the "Odyssey" by matching the numbers in column A with the proper letters in column B:

A	B
1. Odysseus	a. protector goddess
2. Penelope	b. chief of the gods
3. Telemachus	c. son of Odysseus
4. Zeus	d. faithful wife
5. Athene	e. a wanderer

B. Complete the following sentences with the correct word:
1. Charybdis was a dread ....
2. Scylla had .... heads.
3. The land of the dead was called ....
4. Circe turned the men into ....
5. Polyphemus, the ...., had one eye.

C. Make the choice ("a", "b", or "c") which will complete the following statements correctly:
1. Odysseus was returning home from: a. Rome; b. Athens; c. Troy.

2. His home was the island of: a. Troy; b. Ithaca; c. Phaeacia.
3. His men forgot about their homes after eating the: a. daisy; b. poppy; c. lotus.
4. Eurycleia recognized Odysseus, for she had been his: a. wife; b. nurse; c. mother.
5. In a boxing match, Odysseus defeated: a. Eumaeus; b. Irus; c. Antinous.
6. Poseidon made Odysseus' voyage home: a. difficult; b. pleasant; c. speedy.
7. Odysseus lost all of his: a. wealth; b. men; c. arms and legs.
8. Telemachus went searching for his: a. mother; b. brother; c. father.
9. Penelope would not: a. marry; b. live at home; c. accept Telemachus.
10. Peace was restored by: a. Poseidon; b. Argus; c. Athena.

II. Testing Vocabulary (40 points)

A. Choose the best meaning for each of the following words from the five choices given:
1. BRAZEN   a. tall; b. bold; c. strong; d. modest; e. idle
2. RABBLE   a. thief; b. animal; c. mob; d. food; e. dirt
3. PILLAR   a. support; b. soft; c. strike; d. seat; e. medicine
4. COMPROMISE   a. dance; b. engagement; c. agreement; d. company; e. scene
5. PRATTLE   a. toy; b. chatter; c. creature; d. information; e. quarrel

B. Place the following words from the story you have just read in the proper sentences:
a. stratagem; b. assailants; c. majestic; d. insolently; e. gruesome
1. They armed themselves to meet their ....
2. They helped with the .... job of removing the dead.
3. Odysseus' .... had worked.

4. Laertes was stronger and taller, more ....
5. The suitors treated Telemachus ....

C. Match the words in column A with those terms in column B which mean the same, or nearly the same:

A	B
1. inflated	a. fear
2. consoled	b. sympathized with
3. ridicule	c. puffed up
4. dread	d. interfere
5. intervene	e. mockery

D. Match the words in column A with those terms in column B which mean the opposite, or nearly the opposite:

A	B
1. villainous	a. plain
2. elaborate	b. heroic
3. deceptive	c. truthful
4. indignant	d. lose forever
5. retrieve	e. pleased

III. Testing Understanding (20 points)

A. Rearrange the following events as they happen in the story:
1. Odysseus stays with Circe.
2. Odysseus visits his dead mother.
3. The bag of winds is opened.
4. Odysseus escapes the Cyclops.
5. Odysseus meets Eumaeus.

296

The Krown World

THE WANDERINGS OF ODYSSEUS

1. Troy
2. Ciconians
3. Lotus Eaters
4. Cyclops
5. Isle of Aeolus
6. Bag of Winds
7. Laestrygonians
8. Circe's Island
9. Land of the Dead
10. Sirens
11. Clashing Rocks
12. Scylla
13. Isle of the Sun
14. Shipwreck
15. Charybdis
16. Calypso's Island
17. Raft Destroyed
18. Land of the Phaeacians
19. Ithaca